SOFTWARE ENGINEERS DO WHAT NOW?

By Shaun Michael Stone

First Edition UK - 2020

Table of Contents

Creative Commons Notice

Please note: All facts, claims of the use of languages and their industry relevance are based on the time of writing and circumstances can always change.

GitHub - https://github.com/smks

Twitter - https://twitter.com/shaunmstone

YouTube - https://www.youtube.com/c/OpenCanvas

LinkedIn - https://www.linkedin.com/in/shaunmstone

Introduction

"You can't be in the tech community... without
realizing there's a big shortage of talent."

– Mitch Kapor

The tech industry in the UK is thriving. Start-ups, large corporate entities and everything in between are all screaming out for tech specialists in areas of Software, Artificial Intelligence and Financial Tech (FinTech). The UK–especially London–is inhabited with skilful tech-savvy individuals who can bring a lot of innovation to the table. Companies yearn for these individuals, but there's a problem.

The demand doesn't match the supply. There's a lot of jobs out there, therefore, it's a battle for companies to find people–the right skilled people anyway. It's easy to recruit someone, but it's hard to recruit someone who matches the role's requirements. That's why I decided to write this book, to encourage anyone out there who fancies a career change, or is fresh out of University and needs a bit of guidance or direction.

With this book, we will introduce you to the variety of technical roles out there, the positions that exist on the career ladder and make our way through an abundance of sought after technical languages, tools, libraries and frameworks that companies seek. If you are interested in a career in software or just looking to understand the tech side of things, then this is the book for you. Feel free to cherry-pick the bits that interest you more.

End Goal

You will get a feel and basic understanding of the tech that is out there. It may give you a kickstart and the motivation to pursue a career or hobby in software engineering yourself.

This book summarises each of the technologies at a high-level and does not go into real depth. There are *entire* books likely dedicated to each one of them!

Book Coding Style

In this book, you will see code examples in one of the programming languages. What you need to know at this point, is whenever someone creates a source file, it's simply a file on your computer. The file gets opened in a text editor and the developer types letters, symbols and numerical values into this file in such a way that it can be interpreted by the language they are writing in. When the file is saved, it's given an extension to understand what type of source file it is.

```
my-file.js
```

I am giving the file an identity, essentially a passport so anyone who sees it, knows what that file's purpose is. In the example above, it's a JavaScript file.

This book uses examples when working on a Mac and sometimes Windows.

Some of the code examples may wrap onto the next line due to spacing limitations.

Code snippets

When I want to demonstrate to you what is inside a file, I present it in the following way.

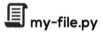 **my-file.py**

This is where I introduce you to what on earth is going on.

```
# start of script
print("hello, hola, ciao");
```

Above is the first bit of code. This is where I bore you with the details of what's going on, or what will happen next.

```
print("goodbye, adios, addio");
# end of script
```

I may or may not show you the output of running the script. Depends if I'm feeling cheeky.

The output will show like so:

```
OUTPUT:
hello, hola, ciao
goodbye, adios, addio
```

All of the code examples can be found in the repository below. Feel free to contribute to this project.

https://github.com/smks/sedwn-code-examples

Prerequisites

1. A Laptop or Desktop

2. Internet access for further research on the technologies

3. Motivation to finish the book. You can do it!

Assumptions

The only thing this book assumes is that you know how to read and put up with my lame jokes. Sorry in advance...

Please note: The book has been designed *not* to expect you to carry out the code examples, but to give you a feel for the subject in question. It may help you understand what area of software you may want to follow or allow you to understand things a bit better when recruiting someone with those specific skills.

Suggestions

You can contact me via any of the social networks if you'd like to give me feedback good or bad (fingers crossed). I'm open to adding or deprecating topics as time goes on for new editions of this book.

- GitHub - https://github.com/smks

- Twitter - https://twitter.com/shaunmstone

- YouTube - https://www.youtube.com/c/OpenCanvas

Or connect with me on LinkedIn for business-related requests.

LinkedIn - https://www.linkedin.com/in/shaunmstone

Also, *please* post a picture with you holding the book. On social media or by email. Regardless, it will *really* make my day! That way, I know it isn't just robots reading it, but actual human beings. Wow, imagine that!

Structure

The book is broken into four parts:

Part 1 - Software Careers

The first part focuses on the software industry ranging from the types of roles out there, recruitment, and what a typical day as a software engineer looks like.

Part 2 - Terminology

The second part is centred around programming and testing terminology used in the industry.

Part 3 - Programming Languages

The third part is a collection of programming languages used by software engineers. This isn't an exhaustive list, but a majority of the most common languages used commercially today.

Part 4 - Web Libraries & Frameworks

The fourth part is focused on web-related libraries and frameworks.

Software careers

PART 1

Here we will observe 'my' career to date, the career paths of individuals in general and take a look at the types of technological roles that are in demand from companies.

- My career experience to date

- Career paths of a software engineer

- The software engineering roles out there

- Agile software development process

- Reasons why software engineers remain at their jobs

- In-depth hiring process of a software engineer

- CV screening tips

- Face to face interview pitfalls

- How tech recruiters stand out

- Learning how to code

My career

> "Choose a job you love, and you will never have to
> work a day in your life."
>
> *– Confucius, Chinese philosopher*

I love the quote above! Before we delve into the book, I wanted to discuss my experience in the tech industry for anyone interested in following the same path. Feel free to skip if it's of no interest to you. I won't be offended. Okay maybe a little bit, but passively.

Hello

My name is Shaun Stone. I'm a Front-end Tech lead from London, UK. I work in the FinTech (Financial Tech) industry. To anyone out there who wants to pursue a career in web development, you may find this useful. I really enjoy what I do, it presents so many challenges I have to tackle. I get to do fulfilling work, mentor and also learn from others, as well as see my work get used by thousands of customers.

Before I applied for a permanent role, I went to University to do a Computing course. When the course finished, I had to do the dreaded job hunt. Why was I so concerned about this? Because I had a degree… but no commercial experience.

To solve this, I started looking for freelance work off my own back, where I would work for next-to-nothing just to get the experience I yearned for. I found some work via Reddit and PeoplePerHour and spent hours working on each project, which I was ecstatic about because I was earning money. On reflection, I would say University helps, but it's not essential.

First role

My first role was at a software house that catered for automotive dealership clients. I started out as a PHP developer and worked on big sites such as Mercedes retail group (was never given a Mercedes unfortunately), Nissan, Mazda and Lookers. Being my first role, I was exposed to a commercial environment, where what I did was vital.

I had to be very articulate and careful with the development work because there was a lot at stake. It essentially threw me into the deep end. The most important thing about this role was that I learned so much from my peers. I was surrounded by smart people I could learn from. A rule I follow is I should always be learning, and if I feel like the smartest person in the room, I'll probably stop learning.

Covent Garden

I decided I wanted to work in London. That was always the plan, so I worked for a finance company based in Covent Garden where I would learn a lot about the financial sector, and I would grow from a Junior into a mid-level PHP developer. Like a Pokémon evolving from a Charmander into a Charmeleon.

I managed high-risk tasks such as sending dynamic emails out to our whole customer base and eventually working on my first User Interface (UI) focused project, which involved rebuilding the customers' web dashboard. It was because of that big project, and it being a great success that I decided I preferred working on the front-end – the visual elements of a web page.

Piccadilly Circus

I moved to a gaming studio company in Piccadilly circus, which was my first front-end development role. It was heavily focused on working hands-on with designers who wanted their designs converted into programmed mini-games. I liked this design-to-development collaboration because things got very creative.

They asked me to implement complex animations a lot which was great as the animation was something I wanted to do as a kid. Because I had a lot of repetitive tasks in general, it inspired me to write a book called 'Automating with Node.js.'

Vauxhall

I now work as a Front-end Tech lead for an investment company in Vauxhall, London. I am involved with recruitment, leading projects, planning meetings and enforcing coding standards/conventions for development across teams. I am also collaborating with the UX/UI/Design team, something I very much enjoy. Woohoo! (Homer impression).

Personal projects

Throughout my career, I've always been busy working on my own hobby projects. This involves writing books and making games or web apps. All of these experiences have helped me grow and understand what's involved so I can foresee technical challenges for other projects I need to tackle. I think it's good to work on things for yourself, for your own self-gratification.

Career path

"Every great developer you know got there by solving problems they were unqualified to solve until they actually did it."

– Patrick McKenzie

Companies have their own roadmap for growth. Similar to my path, a very common pattern of progression as a software engineer is the following.

Please note: *The term developer and engineer are used interchangeably and tend to refer to the same position.*

1 - Junior developer

Junior developers have little-to-no experience. They need to be guided by more senior members of the team to do their work. They usually ask many questions but can learn a lot and are very motivated to do so. Their salary is entry-level. On a side note, companies usually rate your competency level down to the number of years of experience you have. To me, this is a fallacy. I've worked with new starters who were labelled more 'junior' but were knowledgeable and highly competent. Candidates shouldn't always be taken at face value.

2 - Mid-level developer

Mid-level developers have a reasonable amount of experience. They can achieve certain tasks on their own, but still need to look to senior members for guidance from time to time. They can assist juniors and also provide good ideas to senior members but aren't usually willing to lead.

3 - Senior developer

Senior developers can deliver from start to finish with little-to-no guidance. They lead others to do the same and follow good practices. They are experienced enough to know when things can go wrong and how to avoid those problems.

4a - Tech lead/Principal developer

Tech lead/Principal Developer is given to the core/higher rank developer(s) in the team who provides a solid technical vision and has the respect of their peers. Less involved in code, and more so in the foundations of the languages and libraries used, the development process, and the infrastructure.

4b - Team Lead/Team manager

A Team Lead/Team Manager are more focused on the people of the team – their well being, their career progression and having a one-to-one with each team member who reports to them to make sure they are happy but are also delivering as expected. More meetings would result in less development time. It's not an easy task as crucial management skills are required for that.

5 - Technical architect

A Technical architect would overlook the whole structure of the software engineering department. It's mainly around short to long term planning and looking at how to scale the supported systems. Providing documentation on the vision and monitoring the progress of it. They could report to either Engineering managers or the CTO directly.

6 - Engineering manager

An Engineering manager would manage the whole engineering department where Tech leads or Team leads would report to them. But Engineering managers would have a bigger picture of how the department is progressing. They would tend to report to a CTO (Chief Technology Officer).

7 - Chief Technology Officer (CTO)

A Chief Technology Officer is at the top executive level who is focused on the technological issues within the organisation. Examining the short and long term needs and introducing procedures and strategies to drive the company to success.

Flat-based structure

Alternatively, companies employ a more flat-based structure where they remove a lot of the layers described above. Stripping candidates of titles such as Junior/Mid or Senior in favour of a more generic title 'Software engineer.' This, to me, has some pros and cons associated with it.

It can be great for a company because it could work out to be more cost-efficient, require less supervision and dominance across teams. It can also avoid a lot of potential politics.

This is probably ideal for a small company, but as an organisation grows, the management can lose control and decisions can become harder to back up, and if someone wants to feel like they are progressing in their career, the senior job title may help them feel more inclined.

Of course, all of this is subjective and there is no right way proven to work. What matters is that the company figures out what works best for them.

Technology roles

Here we will take a look at the various roles out there for software oriented engineers.

Front-end vs Back-end

It's usually the question linked to inappropriate puns and cheeky grins. "Are you more of a front-end or back-end type?" The person asking the question is, *of course,* referring to the type of technology you work with when they ask this. Duh!

Front-end engineers

> "A front-end web engineer is responsible for implementing visual elements that users see and interact with in a web application."

We are focused on building the UI (User Interfaces) for the users of our website or web application. Things we consider as we work include the following.

Accessibility

Often overlooked on the web, we design our applications to cater for users with some form of disability. This could be some cognitive impairment or limited dexterity. Someone who struggles with clickable areas such as radio inputs or checkboxes is an example. One thing we do is run our UI through a screen-reader (Voice-over utility) to understand how the experience would be for someone who relies on this. A lot of websites do not think about this, which I find very unfortunate.

Aesthetics

The styles of our UI (User Interface) elements such as the colours, buttons, fonts, and spacing are important because we want to abide by our brand and identity.

Performance

We have to think about the performance of our applications to keep page speeds fast. This involves reducing network requests, keeping images optimized using methods like compression. The quicker you load that signup page, the more chance you have of users signing up. We use Lighthouse by Google to benchmark and gather interesting metrics.

Security

Paramount. Tiny bugs in code can result in leaking private information, and there are people out there hungry for it. Of course, it's a huge topic. Search on Google for 'Information Security Basics' by Mozilla.

Quality of code

We use code reviews to check each other's work. We require at least two approvals before anything can proceed to our live applications. We use coding standards that have to be followed across the whole front-end team.

Back-end engineers

"Back-end engineers are software engineers who work on the server components of multi-tier web applications. They focus on web services and the data store (data modelling and databases). They may also be involved with business rule implementation logic."

API

These days back-end developers are responsible for building APIs (Application Programming Interfaces). APIs are built so we can read, create, update or delete data. You might have a Customer API, where we store data around customers, and if we want to get a specific customer's name, their age or address details, the back-end engineer would need to write code to allow us to do so.

Data modelling

Back-end engineers will model a database. A database is a place where data can be stored. They need to make sure it is stored efficiently for quick retrieval. For example, they might create a 'users' table to store information for each user. Each table may have relations to other tables. For example, we may have a transactions table, and we want to retrieve all financial transactions of a specific user.

Documentation

Back-end engineers need to write documentation about the services they build so that others (e.g. Me) can understand how to use it. If I want to get details about a customer for the front-end, I need to be given instructions on how to do so. Documentation is such an important aspect of software development which gets neglected at times.

Back-end security

Yes, 'security' is also paramount on the back-end too. We can't let customers view information about other customers, so back-end engineers have to be careful about the sensitive data they may hold. There is no excuse for inadequate security, especially with critical industries such as Finance or Medicine.

Other specialised engineers

"We all start off as developers, and then call ourselves engineers if we do it for long enough."

There seem to be so many flavours of us these days, must be exhausting for you non-technical lot. This should clarify a few things.

Full-stack engineer

This is an engineer that's capable of doing both front-end and back-end work. It's a common running joke that full-stack engineers are like a drawing of a horse. The back half of the horse is this detailed artistic piece of art, and the front half is a stick figure drawn by a three year old. It's quite a claim to be a master of both, but they do exist I'm sure.

Desktop engineer

This is an engineer that works on software that can be run natively on desktops or laptops. Examples being Mac OS, Windows or Linux. Before the web came along, these were the typical software engineers.

Mobile engineer

Mobile engineers write code for native applications of smartphones and tablets. Native meaning that it's a language accustomed for the operating system it works on. iOS engineers used to build applications with Objective C but now use Swift as standard. Android engineers use Java or Kotlin to build Android applications.

Graphics engineer

Graphic engineers specialise in 2D/3D gaming and video production, taking into account lighting, shading, applying shadow and rendering of models in a 3 Dimensional space. In the early days, it would require a heavy background in advanced math and computer science, but open-source frameworks such as Unity, DirectX and OpenGL make it a lot easier.

Game engineer

Game engineers are of course specialised in the advent of building games. Before Flash was canned, games were built using ActionScript, but now most games are web-based with JavaScript and HTML5 or built as native mobile apps. Game studios who build commercial games use DirectX, OpenGL, Unity 3D, WebGL, and languages such as Java, C or C++ for console and PC releases.

Data scientist

Data scientists are responsible for using data sets for analysis, machine learning and visualising data to understand behavioural patterns or trends in a better way. This is a key area for businesses to become more successful and adaptive.

DevOps engineer

DevOps is shorthand for Development and Operations. DevOps engineers are responsible for providing tools and practices to increase organisations' ability to deliver applications/services at a high velocity. When our front-end and back-end run tests and need a lot of computational resources to carry that out, DevOps can help with this and increase our Time To Market (TTM).

Software development engineer in test (SDET)

This type of engineer is responsible for writing tests for our software systems to see if they operate as expected. They use automated tests and various tools to verify the integrity of another engineer's work.

Embedded systems engineer

These engineers work with the underlying hardware (devices and machines of traditional computers). Examples being consumer electronics, aviation and automotive technology. They would consider things such as temperature and other environmental factors.

Security engineer

A security engineer looks for ways to test the security of a software system to try and identify any flaws. If any vulnerabilities are discovered, it's fixed to avoid a real hacker from trying the same thing. They will build systems or apply manual methods and procedures to do this.

Development process

"Intelligence is the ability to adapt to change."
– *Stephen Hawking*

We – as well as most companies these days – follow the agile principles of software development. Agile software development is claimed as a way to enable teams to deliver faster value, with greater quality and predictability, responding to change more effectively during the process of software development.

Rather than trying to deliver an entire project all at once over a long period of time, it takes the approach of implementing software iteratively through sprints; an iteration of time boxed work ranging from one to four weeks.

The length of a sprint can vary from team to team. What matters is that it works for them. During the process of a sprint, we refine the tickets we have for future sprints.

Backlog

All the remaining work we have is stored in what's called a backlog. This backlog gets filled with work we are to do in the future and is ordered in terms of priority. Having no backlog is definitely a sign that something is wrong and this runs the risk of the team sitting idle.

Having a road-map gives us a clear direction of where we want to be. To do this, we use a project management tool called Jira by Atlassian.

Ceremonies

Ceremonies or 'meetings' are a key part of agile development. It's a way to bring together common goals and an overall vision, share progress across the team and set everyone up for success. Here is a collection of some key ceremonies.

Sprint planning

Sprint planning involves walking through the backlog of work to be done, and prioritizing what should be completed for the sprint. The team has to estimate each story to see how much effort is required by us. Based on the effort involved, we can gauge capacity (how much can be done versus the development resource available).

Stand up

A stand up is a very brief daily meeting with a team where each individual explains what they did yesterday, what they are doing today, and is there anything stopping them from doing their job? (blocking). This keeps everyone in the loop. For each individual, the aim is to keep it short. Once upon a time, a stand up lasted an hour for me. Way too long!

Sprint review

A sprint review happens at the end of the sprint. We showcase to other stakeholders (members of the Product team or users of our system) what we managed to achieve. We do this by giving a demo of the work we have been doing. This gives them confidence that we are progressing.

Retrospective

A retrospective is a way to reflect back on what went well and what didn't. This brings up problems. From those problems, we create actions. An action is an initiated process where we can stop that negative thing from happening again. The things that went well give us an understanding of what makes us work better.

Tech staff retention

> "Salary is usually a driving factor for getting a job, but I think there's much more than that to truly be happy."
>
> *– Me (Shameless plug)*

Please note: *This is my own opinion and not reflective of any company's views.*

Tech companies are always trying to figure out how to keep their employees happy in their jobs. It's no easy feat though, and the people in tech I've spoken to stay at a particular job for around eighteen months or less on average. Whenever I ask any of them what the reason is, it usually stems from the same problems.

Salary is usually a driving factor when choosing a job, but I think there's much more than that to truly be happy. Here are some things I think are important.

Getting along with my manager

They say people don't leave their jobs, they leave their managers. This couldn't be any truer. You should be able to relate to your manager, see eye-to-eye and feel like you can trust one another. Your manager should stick up for you, and you should feel like they are on your side. They should speak to you with respect, dignity and not order you around, abuse their level of control or insult you. Some of the best managers I've had are also great friends of mine to this day.

Management is probably one of the hardest things to do. When I say it's hard, I mean it's hard if you want to be considered a good manager. You need to work extremely hard for your team, manage expectations and keep their morale high. It's not for everyone.

On my first day, my manager introduced me to everyone, organized a team lunch and we all clinked drinks with the words, 'Welcome to the team, Shaun.' I have weekly one-to-one meetings to see how I am doing, if I have any problems, and always feel reassured about the work I do. These are the little things that make a difference.

My ideas and contributions matter

I feel like the ideas other members on the team and I actually push for, do make their way into our applications or our workflow. It may be something to do with the company not being a large corporation, which generally tends to contain a lot of strict regulations for change.

A lot of people get fed up with the fact that they cannot initiate change in a company. Young minds bring fresh ideas that should be embraced, but most of the time, they're not, and that is a shame. When a company has a set way of doing things, it's too risky for them to change because everyone is too comfortable. Companies have to take risks to move forward and innovate.

When young minds feel like they cannot make a difference, they lose their passion and drive for that company. Then they decide to find a job someplace else that will allow them to innovate. Usually, a smaller company such as a start-up gives them that opportunity.

Working from home

We spend most of our lives at work. For me, I commute on the train to London and it takes me approximately fifty minutes door to door.

When I lived with my parents a while ago, I used to commute to London and it took me an hour and forty-five minutes each way. It was horrendous, but I managed to read a plethora of books on my journey. Even every edition of Game of Thrones, so it wasn't a huge waste of time.

My boss at the time said 'you can work from home now and again but of course don't abuse it', which is understandable. A lot of trust is placed on you when you are not in plain sight, but I think allowing you that flexibility when you have to wait at home for the boiler to be fixed by the local plumber is a godsend.

I have found times where working from home actually increased my productivity. I have fewer distractions and it's quiet. I don't need to put on my headphones and I can focus on my tasks much better. The downside is you don't have that real-time in-the-flesh collaboration with colleagues which I think is equally important.

Friendly colleagues

"My colleague once messaged me on Slack... he was sitting next to me."

– A friend

It's a real shame that people in tech get so comfortable staring at that squared energy of light all day without interacting with one another. There have been days where I have done the same because I had deadlines and didn't have time to talk, and I came away that day feeling a bit low. We are naturally social beings, so taking the time out of your day to speak with someone – even about something not related to work – can make you feel better.

We arranged a slack channel for anyone who wants to come to the park with us for lunch and have a good laugh. We arrange nights out in London too with votes on where we should go. Not only that, but we also have a web architecture review meeting for all of the front-end engineers so we can bring up any technical problems we are currently facing in our own teams.

Anyone can bring up a problem or suggest a solution that is then discussed among us all. We then have a vote at the end where everyone is respectful of each other's opinions on the subject.

I'm learning a lot

> "It's what you learn after you know it all that counts."
>
> – *John Wooden*

When we are passionate about our work and the product we are contributing to, we are likely to enjoy our job. We worked on a design system built on a strong foundation of typography, colors, four-pixel spacing, and reusable React components. I loved working on it, and now we are reaping the benefits.

When a developer feels like they aren't learning anything, it could mean that the company is too comfortable and not innovating. The developer is probably doing some maintenance to some legacy code and dealing with the complications of said legacy code. Instead, they could be given the freedom to either find ways to reduce technical debt, identify new solutions to existing problems or work on some exciting new projects where they can work with new technologies to keep their skills sharp. Something that keeps them stimulated.

Development is a fast-paced industry where things are always changing. Especially in front-end! If developers do not feel they are learning new things, they quickly fall behind and consequently become unemployable. It's a reality. They could be an expert in low-level JavaScript fundamentals, but if they don't know how to build a React component, they are seen as unsuitable for the role.

Work recognition

We naturally want to see our company grow, and we want to feel like we are contributing to that growth. Whether it be keeping the servers healthy in DevOps or deploying a fast microservice in the back-end, it's good for someone to identify and appreciate how you helped make it happen.

When colleagues have the mindset that 'well it's your job to do that', it's not healthy for the team. Don't hold back from saying, 'I like how you approached that problem.'

I can dress down

Nothing makes me happier than knowing I don't have to put on a suit every day. Don't get me wrong, I like dressing up and looking 'the business', but it feels good to be in casual clothing and comfortable without a tie trying to strangle me all day.

I'm an engineer. Unless I'm interacting with clients directly, I personally don't see the need to dress up, and worry that my shirt is not ironed. Ironing a shirt every day is such a pain in the backside.

Interview process

Interviews in the technology field are usually not as straightforward as looking at a candidate's CV and then bringing them in for a discussion. It tends to be a multi-step process and the number of steps depends on how big and established the company is.

For a software engineer, it's important that the experience of programming languages, libraries and tools of the candidate match the specific requirements of the job. If a company needs a web engineer with JavaScript experience to help them build websites, then contacting a back-end Java engineer will most likely be a waste of time.

I've been heavily involved in the recruitment process in the last few roles. I work with internal recruiters to help find the right people and provide support throughout the process.

I usually look for people with commercial experience because they will be exposed to a lot of day-to-day problems and will learn on the job, which in my opinion is far more powerful than any coding course or boot camp. As mentioned before, when I didn't have any commercial experience fresh out of University, I did freelance work at a very cheap rate to get it. I then used this in my first development interview to get the job.

Here is a hiring process I think works quite well for a software engineer. *The candidate can potentially drop off at any of the steps below.*

A - CV Review

All candidates stem from either a direct contact – where they've applied to the company directly – or the recruiter has been searching for someone who is not actively looking or unaware of the company's requirement to hire. Either way, both the recruiter and the candidate have to be happy to proceed with the hiring process. The recruiter should be pleased that the candidate has the relevant experience and will be a good fit for the company both technically and culturally, and will use the provided CV to identify the commercial experience.

CV's looking good

If happy with the CV – and running it past the tech team too – a phone call will be initiated where the recruiter will inquire about what the candidate's current situation is and if he is interested in the available role. The recruiter will also identify any constraints such as a working notice period – if they are already in a role at present – and if they have all of the necessary requirements to work in the country. Notice periods are usually a month but can be two or three depending on the contract of the role. Sometimes candidates are immediately available and this can be seen as a huge win.

B - Phone interview

If the candidate is happy about the role, the recruiter will ask a few screening questions provided by the tech team. These questions will be jotted down during the phone call so that they can be reviewed by a technical individual (i.e. A senior software engineer).

If we are happy with the notes of the recruiter, then we, the web team, will have a phone interview scheduled in the calendar. Usually, two of us are involved to bounce off our thoughts. Firstly, we retrieve the details (CV) from our recruitment platform (such as Workable), we check the calendar invite to find out the room we will be calling the candidate from. When calling the candidate, we introduce ourselves and talk about our roles in the organisation.

So... tell me about yourself

We ask them to introduce themselves then move on to general questions about the candidate such as their current situation and what work they have done lately. We delve into their technical knowledge and get a feel for their strengths and weaknesses. When our thirty-minute session is over, we thank them for their time and explain that we will give feedback to our internal recruiter and they will be in touch with the candidate soon.

Positive things we look out for include:

1. Do they understand the technical areas they bring up or are they blagging the answer? (Guessing is a bad thing)

2. Do they ask questions at the end of the call? (Not asking is a huge red flag)

3. Are they actually interested in what we do and the technology we work with?

4. Do they do something innovative that we don't?

5. Are they cultured?

6. Would they be easy to work with? (Extremely important!)

C - Coding test

If we were happy and pass them on the phone interview, the recruiter would send them a technical take-home test. We email them a ZIP folder that contains our coding challenge. This will allow us to demonstrate their ability to code a web application and identify their approach to building it.

Review the test

Ideally, we like it to be done in a week or two. Once they send it back, we review it and score it based on many factors such as code structure, semantics, code quality, pixel perfection, testing and level of effort. If we score them well, then we move on to the next step. We need to measure them on various benchmarks and quantify why we pass or fail them. This reduces our 'gut feeling' decisions.

D - Face to face interview

The final step, and probably the most difficult part of the process, is the face to face interview. It usually lasts three hours, where there will be: two engineers, two senior engineers or a tech lead, and someone from a different department.

1. Hour one - Whiteboarding and simple problem solving

2. Hour two - Review the coding test and get the candidate to walk us through it

3. Hour three - Members of Marketing, Product or Design will check culture fit

After the three hours, there is a group discussion of all parties where we give all of our feedback. It's then a vote for yes or no.

E - Offer of employment

It all comes down to this… negotiation. If the majority of people who interviewed are happy, they will provide their recommendation on what level of expertise the candidate is. This is never a guarantee or accurate representation, but is used mainly as a guidance on the salary side of things.

Offer feedback

Either the offered salary proves to be sufficient or insufficient for the candidate. It's important to match salary expectations with the concrete salary offer otherwise things can go south very fast. Because the demand for engineers is so high, the ball is usually in the candidate's court if they pass the process with flying colours and stand out from the rest.

When time is limited

If time is of the essence, we skip the take-home coding test and bring them over directly for a pair programming session. This means we do the test in real time with them in the same room – as if we were working together on a real problem. This allows us to speed up the process and get an offer out earlier. This doesn't happen often.

CV screening

"Your CV is just a commodity, Package yourself."
– Bernard Kelvin Clive

When someone in the tech industry creates a CV, and they add skills and label keywords of the languages, tools, libraries and frameworks they use, they should be ready to demonstrate that they know them. Anyone can find a list of keywords and throw them on a CV. We jokingly call it 'keyword bingo'. Here are some sections on a CV that I think provides a lot of value.

Personal statement

I usually see this as the main attraction. This summarises everything the candidate has achieved to date and paints a picture for me. It's where they can sell themselves as an individual. I thought I'd use my CV as an example – which I haven't updated for a year or so now. To anyone at my current workplace, I'm happy where I am (wink face).

PERSONAL STATEMENT

Senior Front-end engineer with a passion for improving processes and delivering high-quality end products. To date, I have 7+ years experience building web applications. I've worked in automotive, finance, online gaming and been exposed to building and maintaining bespoke web applications for various companies involved in car valeting, digital entertainment, industrial gases, retailing and broadband comparison services. Some of my key interests involve building high-quality consistent products, writing technical blog articles, teaching, integrating APIs, automating repetitive tasks and building anything considered creative/innovative.

Here, I demonstrate upfront my level of expertise in the field and summarise the industries I've worked in whilst also demonstrating what areas of development I find interesting. For me, it shows that I don't do it just for the money, and I'm genuinely interested and passionate about what I do. I think passion for a job goes a long way and it's possible to identify on a CV whether someone does actually care.

Career achievements

The next section on my CV, I think, quantifies my claim to like automating repetitive tasks, writing blog articles and being creative/innovative. Man, I must sound like such a humblebrag…

CAREER ACHIEVEMENTS

- Author of the book Automating with Node.js - #2 Bestseller on Amazon for JavaScript - June 2018. https://amzn.eu/dcbj90a

- Trending medium blog post on DailyJS with 148,000 total views and 10.2K claps. https://bit.ly/2t6o9JJ

- Worked on an internal presentation web app for IBM using Angular and packaged into an iOS hybrid application using Cordova

- Built automation tool that has saved days of development time using Node.js. Interacts with a JIRA API to scrape values

- Development of an HTML5 Canvas game using Phaser for the UK's most popular online contact lens store

- Creator, Project management, development and design of a children's mobile game released for the web, iOS & Android with C++ native speeds https://bit.ly/2lYnE03

- Working as a freelancer for the largest industrial gas company in North and South America to create a web system that allows employees to choose awards for working with the company

- Development support for a private jet booking application

```
- Provide AXA with an animation tutorial to show interest rates against the
fall in capital value using HTML5 Canvas http://bit.ly/2ujv1p2

- Role-based access control for certain users when arranging valeting services
with well-established car dealerships https://bit.ly/1RSxZE7

- Popular YouTube Channel of technical videos based on web, Operating systems,
OOP and Linux. (14K+ Subscribers & 1mil+ views) https://goo.gl/mzILNc
```

Employment history

I then go on to list my employment history. Without this, I would probably be disqualified for every role. Commercial experience is a huge contributing factor when screening CVs. If a candidate hasn't demonstrated skills in the employment history section, then it's likely that the CV will be disqualified unless the role is for someone more junior. In regards to skills, if I was looking for a job and they required React, Ruby on Rails, I'd be a potential candidate based on the experience outlined below.

```
Senior Front-end engineer 12.17 > Present

COMPANY_NAME | London | COMPANY_WEBSITE

Providing ways of delivering autonomy and ideas to help drive the business
forward. Recruiting other engineers, and making sure the other junior members
of the team achieve their long and short-term goals. Driving the front-end
architecture with a Design System and exposure to React & Redux, AngularJS,
Ruby on Rails, Jenkins and Marathon.
```

Key skills

Finally, I list out the keywords I was referring to at the beginning of this chapter. This is one place where it lists out all of the languages, tools, libraries and frameworks I've claimed to use at some point in my career. I have to be ready to talk about any of them in any part of the hiring process.

KEY SKILLS

```
HTML5, SASS/CSS, JavaScript, Typescript, PHP 5/7, Docker, MySQL, Haxe, Git,
SVN, Gulp, WebPack, Bash, Responsive design, Photoshop, Illustrator.
Angular 1 & up, React & Redux, Laravel, Phaser, EaselJS, HaxeFlixel, Cordova &
PhoneGap.
```

CV considerations

If you're in a position of reviewing CVs, take note of the things below when making your decision. Alternatively, if you are writing a CV to apply for a role, try and avoid these potential flags.

1. The CV doesn't list the correct skills required (Unqualified)

2. The CV glosses over the gaps in their employment history

3. Littered with spelling errors. *It's a compromise if English is not their first language*

4. The dates are inaccurate

5. It's hard to read

6. Poorly formatted

7. Their achievement claims are debunked

8. Has no references

9. Uses cliché

10. Job title inflation. *E.g. The only developer in a business claiming to be a Tech Lead or Architect*

11. Lack of a coding portfolio

12. Listing irrelevant certifications achieved a decade ago

Interview pitfalls

"I think it's best not to identify the weaknesses, but instead, identify the strengths of a potential candidate."

– Me (Shameless plug)

As a Recruiter, it can be frustrating when an interview doesn't go as per the plan and falls short of expectations. Sometimes it can be a misunderstanding of either party involved. To be a bit biased, I will talk from the perspective of an engineer going through an interview process where things can fall through, but it may not be the case that the engineer was a bad fit for the role, it's that the interviewer was potentially at fault by not identifying the true strengths of the candidate.

Complexity of role

I've had discussions with many friends about a few of their experiences in technical face to face interviews. Some went well, some went bad, and some were just outright ridiculous. You see, sometimes an interview goes wrong, and it's not always the fault of the candidate. This person may be considered the creative/visual type, with strong expertise in building solid UI elements that can be used in web applications, but then gets asked in the interview how to solve a complex algorithm around binary trees or big O on a whiteboard. *These are terms used in Computer Science.*

This question — not always — may be valid for a data scientist at a place like Facebook or Google, but most of the time, a job doesn't require such complexity on a daily basis.

Qualities that matter

> "People who think they know everything really annoy those of us who know we don't"
>
> — *Bjarne Stroustrup - Creator of C++*

The job probably involves building common sense features for an existing web application that applies: solid communication with stakeholders, clean, tested and well-organised code, and the incorporation of strong web standards involving accessibility. In the end, code gets shipped by them without complications and gets delivered in a timely manner.

These qualities are so vital in a role and don't usually get identified during the interview process. The interviewers are more interested in trying to make the candidate look stupid, to find loopholes in their knowledge, or just to fulfil their own sense of pride. The mindset of, 'I know this, but does he?' You know what? Maybe they don't know, and it's okay not to know everything. Not everyone does.

Company domain knowledge

Companies also have their own domain knowledge, which means, internally, they are familiar with their own terminology, how things work or operate and are accustomed to the common problems they face. These problems could be extremely simple to an internal employee, but for someone coming in from the outside? Not so much!

So interviewers should try and see things from the interviewee's perspective. The interviewer may talk about a problem he is currently facing and ask the candidate how we would go about solving it. Likely the candidate will look like a deer in headlights.

I think it's best not to identify the weaknesses, but instead, identify the strengths of a potential candidate. What do they have that we might be lacking? Do we have an expert in CSS who can simplify some of our rules? Was their previous role more marketing-focused, which means they know Google Tag Manager like the back of their hand? Do they know React at a deep level or can identify performance issues we never considered? Someone who has strong DevOps knowledge that can help us build robust Jenkins pipelines for some of our packages?

Candidate strengths over weaknesses

There is more to a candidate than identifying if they know how to flatten a multi-dimensional array, what a prototype chain or closure is. Are they approachable and helpful to others? Can they leave pride at the door and do what's best for the team? Can they explain technical requirements in laymen's terms to stakeholders? Do they keep everyone in the loop — who may be affected by the changes they are planning to make?

If you cannot see any potential in the candidate and you feel the technical knowledge is not there, then yes, maybe it's best not to proceed, but don't rule someone out just because they couldn't figure out a problem on a whiteboard. Check the quality of their code test, the way they came across in the interview, the problems they solved in previous roles — the bigger picture. You'll be surprised at how many talented people in the industry have — and still do — get turned down.

Experts in field turned down

Kyle Simpson, the author of 'You don't know JS,' was turned down by a big social network company for 'not knowing JavaScript.' His JavaScript books are considered some of the best books on the topic and are best-sellers. Max Howell, who created Homebrew, which is used by 90% of Google employees, was turned down at Google for not knowing how to do a binary tree on a whiteboard.

In all seriousness, having a poor interviewing process reflects very badly on the company. If a candidate has a negative experience, they will feed Glassdoor some juicy details. Some of the biggest and most successful companies have huge flaws in these areas, and it's wrong to think that just because the company is doing well that they should leave things as they are. There is always room for improvement.

Tech recruiters

> "Don't treat a candidate like a number, instead treat them like a person that has distinct needs in a new role. Be attentive to their requirements and set expectations right away."
>
> *– Me (Shameless plug)*

This is a chapter dedicated to tech recruiters. I've had my fair share of interaction with recruiters over the years, and I know recruitment gets a bad rap. It's a shame because I know there are so many good ones out there, but unfortunately, there are a lot of bad ones too that make it a numbers game and are just in it for the money. I imagine it's frustrating as a recruiter. First off, it's extremely competitive and saturated, then you must consider what else they have to deal with; the myriad of disappointments around candidates choosing other offers, candidates avoiding phone calls or not even turning up to interviews.

Positives of recruitment

On the plus side, it pays seriously well in most cases. They get to help people's careers and build strong connections as they mature. I've seen shared images of recruitment agencies on the social scene, and it looks like a lot of fun after a long day at work. On the other side of the fence, if you are going into the tech market as a software engineer, prepare to get very popular. As soon as you post your CV on a job board, your phone will be ringing more than my historic spells of tinnitus.

Here are a few positive things that I think make a recruiter stand out from… the millions (The Rock reference).

Innovative job descriptions

I always find it interesting how recruiters pitch their roles on a web platform such as LinkedIn. Sometimes they can get quite innovative by posting jokes or small brain teasers. It definitely catches my attention, and it allows the recruiter to get creative. Candidates will likely scan a post for a few seconds, so the recruiter needs to make it clear and concise about what they are offering. Adding a bit of humour or mystery around it makes it more appealing.

Get to the point

Candidates want to know what work they will be doing, what perks they get, the location, and, of course, how much money they will make. I also think this applies when a recruiter makes a call to a candidate. Attention spans are so short these days, and that long-winded questionnaire at the beginning of the call makes a candidate want to cut the call ASAP – especially if they are calling during working hours. Talking for ten minutes to then find out the candidate is not even interested in the role is a waste of everyone's time.

Be honest & genuine

Getting called 'Fella' or 'Brother' doesn't come across very well on the first phone call. Do you trust that I'm well? Thanks! Wow! This recruiter has this: amazing, disruptive, innovative, ground-breaking, trendsetting, once-in-a-lifetime opportunity. Meh! All recruiters say that these days, and it's lost its prestige. It's become a noisy sales pitch.

Cut the BS

Make it something more concrete and meaningful like, 'This FinTech company is migrating its entire legacy PHP codebase to React and implementing a micro front-end architecture so they can offer a Software as a Service (SAAS) product. They are facing a lot of technical challenges with X, Y and Z and would need someone like you to help them work it out.' We love solving problems! A web developer with React experience would jump at the chance to be part of something like this—considering every other aspect of the role is sufficient.

Don't treat a candidate like a number, instead treat them like a person that has distinct needs in a new role. Be attentive to their requirements and set expectations right away. If a recruiter sells them this job role where everything is perfect, it will make the candidate sceptical, and they'll lose trust in their words.

Say it how it is

No company is perfect! There are always challenges that have to be tackled. Let them know that they will be obligated to work on a few other legacy applications, or do their fair share of QA and product discovery alongside their normal responsibilities. At least they'll know what to expect. If they don't find that out during the call, they will find out later and leave anyway if it's a deal-breaker.

Agency vs Product-focused roles

In my experience, there are usually two types of job roles that require different mindsets. There are design agency roles where projects stream through fast like an overflowing river where everything is rushed out of the door with countless last-minute changes to satisfy a client. On the other side of the spectrum is the product-focused role where there's more of a spotlight on quality, building foundations, and processes of a single offering.

If a candidate makes an effort to attend interviews or do code tests, regardless of the outcome, keep the communication strong. Don't scream at them if they decide the role offered is not for them. It's their career, after all. That's happened to me before and it wasn't nice.

Done their research

There's nothing more irritating than when I get contacted about a role that has no relevance to what I do. No, I don't want to be a Junior Windows IT Support Technician in Hull or a Pet food taster. Okay, maybe I went too far with that example.

Check that spec

Before contacting an individual, check the job specification and see if it matches up with their CV or LinkedIn profile. How many years of experience do they have? If they've just started their career, then companies looking for a mid-level or senior with some substantial commercial experience would likely not be interested.

Learning to code

"One of the best programming skills you can have is
knowing when to walk away for awhile."

– Oscar Godson

Anyone can code if they put their mind to it. Yep, I said it. It's always
perceived as something really difficult. If you invest time to
understand it, build things and identify problems early, you will grow,
become less frustrated and eventually see the fun/rewarding side of it.

Good skills to have

Some good skills to have as a programmer:

1. Patience - Have the tenacity to keep working through challenges

2. Inventive - Thinking of better/faster ways to work effectively

3. Problem-solving - Think through solutions and choose the best
    one

4. Communication - To avoid mistakes, speed up development and
    increase morale

5. Collaboration - Innovation is so much better when working as a
    team

6. Persistence - Don't let problems defeat you, keep going

7. Humility - Be receptive to criticism and other people's ideas

8. Helpful - Help others having issues, even if they are
    obvious/overlooked

9.   Adaptive - The tech world changes quite fast, keep learning

10. Respectful - Don't rewrite your teammate's code without a discussion beforehand

Ways to learn to code

There are two ways of learning, and both are equally as important.

A - Reading about code

When you open up a book on a train and flick through the pages of code examples and nod your head to say, 'Aha, so that's how you do that thing', you're building up your understanding of that language on an intellectual level only.

Reading alone is not enough. If an employer sat you in front of a computer, you would not know what on earth to do, even if you had read ten books on the subject. Musicians can't learn their instruments without playing the darn thing over and over again, and this brings us onto 'acting on code.'

B - Acting on code

When you are at home on a laptop or PC, and you have a text editor open, and you actively follow along by writing the code of a book or online course and confirm what you've written in the editor works, you are building up knowledge through the repetition of keystrokes.

When something in your code fails and you are sitting there scratching your head in dismay, but you eventually work out what went wrong, if it happens again, you know how to tackle it, making you wiser and more experienced. This sums up my career in a nutshell, to be honest.

In my experience, I tend to read books on theory. But any new programming languages or libraries I need to know, I will act on learning material by writing out the examples. Theory can be applied to any programming language.

The games I've built in the past would introduce fresh new problems that I'd never come across before. The experience I've gained on personal projects on how to code is phenomenal.

The next steps

Once you have finished this book, ask yourself the following questions. Hopefully, this book will give you the answers to head in that direction. If not, then I have work to do in the next edition.

1. What area of programming interests you?

2. What type of responsibilities would you want in a role?

3. What industry interests you? Gaming? Data science? UI development?

4. What language caught your interest?

5. Where do you want to go with your career?

Terminology

There are so many blooming terms in the world of software. It's no wonder people get so confused. In this part, we will cover some terminology you may have heard and always wondered *what on earth* it meant.

- Software Development Terminology

- Software Testing Terminology

Software development terminology

Here's a not-so-exhaustive list of common terms you may hear around an office full of tech-heads.

API (Application Programming Interface)

Think of an API as something that businesses build to provide a form of service to their customers or business partners. Similar to the real world, you want a carpenter to build you a chair. Up front you detail what you need to be a happy customer, and the carpenter does all the work behind the scenes to deliver what you want.

The same is said in the digital world. If you have your own online store and you want to have a custom-designed map on your website so your customers can find you easier, then you likely wouldn't build a map from scratch, you'd perhaps use an existing API – such as Google Maps to do this.

Asynchronous & Synchronous

When you execute a task synchronously, you wait for it to finish before moving on to another task. However, when you execute something asynchronously, you can move on to another task before the initial task finishes. Let's say you made five API calls, each retrieving different data. Running all of these tasks asynchronously could likely result in faster completion of all tasks.

If you did them synchronously, you would do API call #1, wait for it to finish, then move on to API call #2, and so on. This is something we consider when building front-end applications where we need data to populate the values on a web page. To speed up requests, we make our network requests asynchronous.

Caching

This is what happens when you've originally requested a resource – such as an image. Rather than downloading the image all over again when you refresh the page, it's stored in the browser (browser cache) to reduce the overheads of downloading it again from its original location.

CDN (Content Delivery Network)

A CDN is a network of computers that delivers content to users. They are positioned geographically to serve the user requesting the content faster. So if I'm in the UK but access a website based in the USA, a server will be located closer to me to deliver content more efficiently across the wire.

You may use a CDN to store image assets for a web page, but more significant use cases could be 4K or HD quality videos, audio, apps or games. Without having a CDN, a website with high traffic of users *may* struggle to keep up with the requests.

CI/CD (Continuous Integration/Continuous Deployment)

As developers, when we commit our code, we want to run some checks on it to make sure it works correctly. We strive to ship code that works, even if it's a tiny change. We run tests on our code to make sure it works and these tests are triggered once our code has been pushed. These tests are part of a bigger process, a pipeline.

A pipeline is a series of steps/checks on our code. If all of these steps succeed, it's considered a pass, where it'll give us the green light to deploy to production. If it fails, we are informed that it's not acceptable to deploy our code changes. These frequent, successful iterative code changes are 'continuously integrated' into our main codebase(s). It's an automated process that watches for changes on our codebase and when a change is detected, it runs the checks and passes or fails us.

Continuous Deployment incorporates CI - where it can automatically release code that has passed through the pipeline where it's then accessible for end-users – without human intervention. Although this is configurable by the operators (DevOps team). It's a way to release software continuously or as often as possible.

CMS (Content Management System)

There have been times in my career where a marketing employee would want to make a change to some landing page of a website, but they had to go through a software engineer who would have to make a manual code change, test, then release it. This process is very slow and inefficient. Text changes are a frequent requirement and it makes no sense for a software engineer to waste time on such a controversial task.

Content management systems give the control of changing visual content over to the non-technical people where they can publish changes themselves using an authorised back-end system. WordPress is an example of a Content Management System built for bloggers, where you can add pages, blog posts, images and more without having to write code. You can if you want to, though.

CRM (Customer Relationship Management)

CRM is a technology used to manage customer – or potential customer – interactions. CRM is considered a strategy for a business or a process to manage customer-business relations, but is used primarily as a software product to provide bespoke/relevant information to customers or record interactions made by customers to better understand them.

These tools would be mainly used by a Marketing or Sales team to do their job more effectively. However, CRM can be used in other unconventional ways such as a Human Resources team tracking employee performance.

Cookies

Cookies are a great tasting snack. But in computing terms, a web/Internet/browser cookie is a small piece of stored data that persists for a set period of time on the user's device/machine. A cookie may be used to keep track of visits or items of a shopping basket.

If you went to a new page and didn't have data persisted on that page, you'd lose all of your shopping items. Not good! When you see those annoying consent pages pop up on a website and click 'Agree,' you are consenting to store the cookies of that website in your browser.

Framework + Library

You may hear the term framework a lot in the software world. A framework is simply a set of tools put together to make your life a bit easier when coding. Technical challenges that you would otherwise have to think about yourself and spend time on are solved for you with frameworks. Well, in most cases.

How this differs to a library is that the framework has set most of the foundations for a coding project. This means you have to spend time learning how the framework functions and it locks down the way you work.

A library and framework often get confused with one another and are used interchangeably. A library and framework are both pieces of code written by someone else and both help you solve common problems.

Let's use an analogy of building a theme park. The framework would dictate the way I build each ride and how everything communicates. If I wanted one specific ride to do something extra like add flashing lights and quirky music, I'd use a library to provide this extra functionality – something the framework likely doesn't provide out of the box.

HTTP Status Codes

When we as developers make any form of network request, we will get an HTTP status code back for every request. This status code will vary depending on the circumstances. Each code has an associated meaning. 'XX' can be replaced for many variations of the same categories outlined below.

1. 1XX - Informational (100, 101, 102)

2. 2XX - Success (Everything was fine) (200, 201, 202)

3. 3XX - Redirection (We decided to take you somewhere else) (301, 302)

4. 4XX - Client Error (You did something wrong) (400, 401, 404)

5. 5XX - Server Error (We did something wrong) (500, 502)

To learn more about these status codes, check out HTTP response status codes at https://developer.mozilla.org.

IDE (Integrated Development Environment)

Think of a text editor like Notepad. It has nothing but black and white text, and it allows you to type characters into it. Now, think of an IDE, a text editor on steroids that allows developers who write code, where it provides feedback on whether you are writing code correctly, predicting what you are typing ahead, debugging your code, building your code, and colouring your code to make it easier to interpret. That is an IDE. Shout out to the 'Visual Studio Code' IDE for being the best one on the market for me.

Plugin/Extension

A plugin or extension is an optional piece of software code that can be 'plugged in' to existing technology. For instance, back in the day when you wanted to stream videos or Flash games, you would have to install a plugin to support the running of this media.

Object Oriented Programming (OOP)

Object-oriented programming is a style of coding that isolates real-world objects into their own classes (A blueprint of many possible objects).

When an architect thinks of building a house, he/she doesn't create it straight away. They create a plan of how to shape that house, and if it's a solid blueprint, they could use it as the basis to create as many houses as they'd like. The same applies to classes and objects. A class is a blueprint of one or many objects.

Responsive Web Design

This is a practice that allows you to adapt the web page based on different mobile, TV, and tablet devices as well as desktops. If your web page looks presentable in each screen view (known as a breakpoint), then it's considered 'responsive.'

Sequential vs Concurrency vs Parallelism

A - Sequential

Let's imagine Lionel the Lion (The animal on the front cover) with a single juggling ball in his possession. Whenever he throws that ball in the air and then catches it with the same paw, he'll earn a one pence coin. So he throws it up and down ten times and earns ten pence. He loves the fact he's earning money! The problem with one juggling ball is this sequential process is quite slow. So he picks up an additional four balls to speed up his earnings.

B - Concurrency

Now in phase two, again using a single paw, he throws and catches the five balls with four consistently in the air. He's managing these juggling balls **concurrently**.

C - Parallelism

Lionel asks his family to help him juggle more balls at the same time so they can earn *even more* money. So greedy! **Parallelism** is the family of lions juggling their own set of balls at the same time.

Imagine each ball is a user who is requesting a web page. We want to manage as many user requests at the same time to keep the user from waiting too long. We want to serve them as quickly as possible. Concurrency and Parallelism are methods on how to deal with this load more efficiently.

Terminal/Console

A terminal is an interface in which you can type special commands and execute them to get the desired result. For example, if I was on a

MacBook and wanted to know what my present working directory (PWD) is.

```
pwd
```

Then hit enter, it would execute the 'pwd' command and give me back what I asked for; the path of my current directory.

```
'/Users/shaun/projects/my-app'
```

UI (User Interface)

The User Interface is anything a user can interact with. This falls to the UI designers who decide on colour themes and shapes of elements such as forms, buttons along with all the various states, panels, and icons. They take transitions, animations and any micro interactions into consideration to give a nice feel to the user consuming it.

The UI designer creates something in line with the brand and identity of the product they work on. It's up to the UI designer to make the user's interface attractive, modern and consistent.

UX (User Experience)

The User Experience (UX) is determined by how users interact with the application. Does the flow feel seamless to the user? Do they do it without frustration? Is the user accomplishing the task they set out to do? These are the questions that UX designers consider, and are usually feedback-driven by doing user testing and identifying/addressing anything that makes the user frustrated.

UI and UX both deal with the user interface. The main difference is that the UI designers decide how the user interface will look, whilst the UX designer will determine how the user interface will work.

Version Control

Version control is an essential part of the software development process. It's a way to manage code more effectively by keeping track of history and separating code of developers so they can work in isolation.

Have you ever worked on the same document as a few other people and tried to save the file, but someone else has just saved it too. It's hard working on the same thing without conflicts occurring. Version control avoids the problem of file locking and having to create many files of the same content. Seen this before?

```
BobsSpeech.docx
BobsSpeechFinal.docx
BobsSpeechFinalFinal.docx
BobsSpeechFinalFinal2.docx
BobsSpeechFinalFinal3.docx
```

It's always the final, isn't it, Bob? Almost all software projects use version control to manage versions of the source code. Because many developers might work on the same file, they can by creating a 'branch' and doing their work in isolation without interfering with someone else's version/branch.

```
master
  bobs-branch
  clives-branch
```

Now they have their own versions and can save as much as they like. When both are finished, they can 'merge' their changes to the master branch. The master branch can be defined as the main version that everyone regards as the single source of truth.

```
master << bob's and clive's changes get merged to make a single file
```

Git is the de-facto (Version Control System) used commercially.

Software Testing Terminology

This is a collection of functional testing approaches that can – and should – be applied to our software development process. Without testing our code, if we made code changes later on and released those changes to production, we wouldn't know how our changes have impacted other areas of the codebase, and this is very risky. Working somewhere that 'doesn't have time' for adding tests is a *huge* red flag.

Unit Testing

Unit testing is a low-level test of your code. It breaks down the code into tiny pieces that get tested in isolation. If I have a function that adds two numbers together, I expect that function to return the total correctly.

 add.js

```
function add(a, b) {
  return a + b;
}

module.exports = add;
```

 add.test.js

```
const add = require("./add");

describe("add", () => {
  it("should add two numbers", () => {
    expect(add(1, 2)).toBe(3);
  });
});
```

If this fails, we can pinpoint where in our codebase it fails and we then correct our 'add' function.

```
function add(a, b) {
  return a - b; // made an accidental change that WILL fail
}
```

When we make the accidental change above and run the unit tests, it will flag this small unit of code is invalid, as seen below.

```
OUTPUT:

add > should add two numbers

Expected: 3
Received: -1

Tests: 1 failed, 1 total
```

Integration Testing

Integration testing is a level of software testing that combines units of code together to see how they integrate. If three teams worked on three different components of a car, you would have to see how those components integrate. Do they work well and compliment each other? The same applies to software.

Example 1

1. Does the car turn on?

2. Do the lights come on when I turn on the car?

Example 2

1. Can I accelerate?

2.   Does it flag that I haven't put my seatbelt on as I accelerate?

Don't try this at home, kids!

System/End to end Testing

This is testing as a whole. Can every single component of a Car operate as expected together? Let's check by doing an end to end test. Can I complete a journey in the car when starting from destination A and finishing at destination B? If something fails at any point of that journey, then the 'end to end' test will fail.

An example for me at my company – if onboarding a new customer, can they fill in all of their personal details and create an investment pot successfully? We need to ensure this is possible with the latest version of our code before releasing it to our customers.

Sanity Testing

Sanity Testing is performed after the software has been pushed for testing to check that minor changes – that were originally a bug/issue before – have been dealt with as expected. This saves time and costs where, if verified, would proceed to a more rigorous testing phase.

Smoke Testing

Smoke Testing is performed after the software has been pushed for testing to ensure the critical functions of the program are working as expected. Can the user log in? Can they view their dashboard? Can they subscribe to a new product? If something is caught early, it can be rejected more efficiently.

Regression Testing

Regression Testing is done to make sure that existing working features of software work like they did before when introducing new changes to the existing software. If you could log in before, but now you can't since the latest code change was released, then this is considered a regression.

Acceptance Testing

Acceptance testing is where a system/application is tested against the requirements initially outlined by the stakeholder. If a developer was asked to make a button green, but they made it turquoise, then this would fail the Acceptance Criteria (AC). You can have internal testing that is performed by internal members of the business, or external testing where third parties outside of the company do it.

Languages

PART 3

Here we will delve into the wondrous world of coding languages. This is not a list of every language on the planet (I'd never finish this damn book), but enough to give you an idea of what is out there on the market. The coding language – or languages – chosen by a developer will shape their future role and career. Usually, when a programmer starts a job, they are allocated a language (or a handful of languages) they specialise in.

Each chapter will have the following sections and use code examples of the standard library:

- Language introduction

- Code example

- Use cases

- Did you know?

HTML

Language introduction

Don't listen to Quagmire. It actually stands for Hypertext Markup language. HTML is not a programming language. Instead, it's known as a 'Markup' language. Every document of HTML can be one of many connections to other web pages with the use of hyperlinks.

Consider building a shed, HTML will be the foundation of this shed: The wood boards, the arch-top windows, flooring and roof.

When you write some HTML markup, you are constructing a collection of tags. Here is an example of a tag.

Code example

```
<p>Sup</p>
```

In this example, we are creating a paragraph, and inside the tags we are saying, create a paragraph with the content 'Sup.'

This 'p' tag isn't just some random letter. It's one of many official tag elements supported by the web. If you want to create a paragraph of text, you should write a 'p' tag and put your text inside it.

Every piece of markup in an HTML file has a start and end tag to tell the browser, "hey, my tag is starting," and "hey, my tag is finishing/closing."

So when I want to start writing a paragraph, I begin by typing the starting tag.

```
<p>
```

Next, I write the paragraph content.

```
Java is to JavaScript what ham is to hamster.
```

Once I want to finish the paragraph, I close it.

```
</p>
```

The character '/' is used to tell the browser this tag is a closing tag. An HTML file is a large collection of these tags. Let's see an example of a HTML document.

 **index.html**

```
<html>
  <head>
    <title>
      My title
    </title>
  </head>
  <body>
    <!-- header -->
    <header>
      <!-- header content goes here -->
      <h1>Header</h1>
    </header>
```

```
<nav>
  <!-- main navigation goes here -->
</nav>
<!-- page's main content -->
<main>
  <!-- an article -->
  <article>
    <h2>Article heading</h2>
    <!-- article content -->
  </article>
  <aside>
    <h2>Related</h2>
    <!-- aside content goes here -->
  </aside>
</main>
<!-- footer -->
<footer>
  <!-- footer content goes here -->
</footer>
</body>
</html>
```

Use cases

Front-end developers and designers use HTML heavily for:

1. Creating web pages that are displayed on the world wide web

2. Creating documents on the web

3. Navigating the web

4. Storing data in the browser

5. Offline usage (If the internet cuts out)

Did you know?

- It's vital to use the correct HTML tags so that screen-readers and other tools (used by people with some form of disability) have a better understanding of the content they are navigating.

- Tim Berners-Lee and Robert Cailliau changed the world forever. Robert, along with Tim, developed the hypertext system for accessing documentation and built the first ever web server

- "Tim was a graduate of Oxford University, Sir Tim invented the Web while at CERN, the European Particle Physics Laboratory, in 1989. He wrote the first web client and server in 1990. His specifications of URIs, HTTP and HTML were refined as Web technology spread." w3.org/People/Berners-Lee

CSS

Language introduction

CSS is an abbreviation for Cascading Style Sheets. It's used to target elements on a webpage and apply specific styles to those elements. If I wanted to change the text colour of a paragraph from the default of black to a blue, I would use CSS to do so.

CSS is one of the core languages of the open web. The specifications of CSS are maintained by a group called the World Wide Web Consortium (W3C). CSS has a lot of features, but they vary in browser support. A developer has to first check if the feature is a W3C Recommendation – meaning it's safe to use.

Code example

```
p {
  color: blue;
}
```

CSS is a great friend to HTML because it separates structure and presentation. HTML dealing with the former and CSS the latter. Using the analogy of building a shed where HTML is the structure - door, windows, floorboards, CSS would be the exterior designer that can increase/decrease the width of the door, paint the shed with a colour of choice, or angle the roof.

CSS can turn the boring dull shed into something spectacular. Why don't we build a shed now? I'm really glad you asked!

shed.html

```
<html>
  <head>
    <link rel="stylesheet" href="shed.css" />
  </head>
  <body>
    <section class="container">
      <div class="shed">
        <div class="roof"></div>
        <div class="door"></div>
      </div>
    </section>
  </body>
</html>
```

Here's an example of some CSS code. We are targeting tags above so we can style them using classes.

shed.css

```
:root {
  --outline-size: 30px;
  --shed-color: #ffad61;
  --door-color: #795548;
  --outline-color: black;
  --shed-height: 500px;
  --shed-width: 600px;
  --door-height: 400px;
  --door-width: 300px;
  --roof-angle: 100px;
  --roof-height: 150px;
}

.shed {
```

```css
  background-color: var(--shed-color);
  border: var(--outline-size) solid var(--outline-color);
  height: var(--shed-height);
  position: relative;
  width: var(--shed-width);
}


.door,
.roof {
  position: absolute;
}


.door {
  background-color: var(--door-color);
  border: calc(var(--outline-size) / 1.5) solid var(--outline-color);
  border-bottom: none;
  bottom: 0;
  box-sizing: border-box;
  height: var(--door-height);
  left: calc(50% - calc(var(--door-width) / 2));
  width: var(--door-width);
}


.roof {
  border-color: var(--outline-color) transparent;
  border-style: solid;
  border-width: 0 var(--roof-angle) var(--roof-height) var(--roof-angle);
  left: calc(var(--roof-angle) * -1);
  top: calc(var(--roof-height) * -1);
  width: var(--shed-width);
}


.container {
  display: flex;
  align-items: center;
  justify-content: center;
  height: 100vh;
}
```

If I open 'shed.html' up in the browser, it renders a beautiful shed. Isn't it everything you've ever dreamed of?

Sass/Scss

Sass (Syntactically awesome style sheets) is a way to extend the limitations of CSS to manage styling in a better way. It will then compile down to CSS during the web app build process. It gives you things such as variables, nesting styles inside of other styles, importing other Sass files and a thing called mixins, which allows you to write more efficient and reusable CSS.

📃 **example.scss**

```scss
// import other Sass code
@import "reset";

// variable
$my-color: black;

// nesting
.parent {
  border: 1px $my-color solid;
  .child {
    background-color: $my-color;
```

```
    width: 20%;
  }
}

// function you can reuse
@mixin border-radius($radius) {
  -webkit-border-radius: $radius;
  -moz-border-radius: $radius;
  -ms-border-radius: $radius;
  border-radius: $radius;
}

.box {
  @include border-radius(10px);
}

.box-2 {
  @include border-radius(5px);
}
```

When the script above is run through a web build process, it generates the following CSS.

📄 **example.css**

```
/* 'reset' styles imported here **/

.parent {
  border: 1px black solid;
}

.parent .child {
  background-color: black;
  width: 20%;
}

.box {
  -webkit-border-radius: 10px;
  -moz-border-radius: 10px;
  -ms-border-radius: 10px;
  border-radius: 10px;
```

```
}
.box-2 {
  -webkit-border-radius: 5px;
  -moz-border-radius: 5px;
  -ms-border-radius: 5px;
  border-radius: 5px;
}
```

Use cases

CSS is used to style web pages, so it's an important aspect of UI development for any website or web application.

- Front-end developers

- Web designers

- Full-stack developers

- UI developers

Did you know?

- In the 1990s, before CSS was adopted as the standard, there weren't many options to layout content on a web page.

- CSS was first proposed in 1994 by a Norwegian web pioneer named Håkon Wium Lie. He worked with Tim Berners-Lee and Robert Cailliau at a company called CERN

- According to https://www.w3.org/Style/CSS/all-properties.en.html CSS supports over 520 distinct properties, ranging from Editor's draft (Not submitted yet) to a 'Recommendation of use' from W3C

JavaScript

"Any app that can be written in JavaScript, will eventually be written in JavaScript."

– *Jeff Atwood, Software developer*

Language introduction

No, this is not Java! This is JavaScript. They are different, trust me. If you are a recruiter, do not make this mistake on the phone to a programmer. They will roll their eyes so fast that they will fall out, resulting in a difficult career in programming.

JavaScript is a scripting/programming language that allows you to add functionality to web pages. If we used HTML and CSS alone on a website, you wouldn't have much interaction going on in your pages.

Going back to the example of a shed. If HTML is the structure of the shed, and the CSS is to make the shed look vibrant – and make the neighbours jealous, then how does JavaScript come into it?

Code example

Think of JavaScript as a way to make the shed interactive. If I press a button on my remote control, the door should open if it is closed, and close if the door is open. In this example, we can press the spacebar on our keyboard to open and close the door.

📑 remote-control.js

```javascript
// set a boolean variable (can be either true/false)
let doorIsOpen = false;
const SPACE_BAR = 32;


function closeDoor() {
  // this code block will run only if we call closeDoor();
  doorIsOpen = false;
  alert("closed door");
}


function openDoor() {
  // this code will run only if we call openDoor();
  doorIsOpen = true;
  alert("opened door");
}


// when we press on the spacebar key this code will run
const onPress = function(e) {
  // don't open or close the door if the key
  // was NOT the space bar
  if (e.keyCode !== SPACE_BAR) {
    return;
  }

  // if the door is open
  if (doorIsOpen) {
    // we will close the door
    closeDoor();
  } else {
    // otherwise we will open the door
    openDoor();
  }
};


// add a listener for any key press
const remoteControl = window.addEventListener("keypress", onPress);
```

Use cases

- Front-end developers

- Full-stack developers

- Back-end developers (Node.js)

JavaScript is popular for a reason. It's used for:

1. Web development

2. Web applications

3. Presentations

4. For back-end and web servers (PayPal's whole back-end systems are built with it)

5. Games are built in it

6. Used for Smartwatch applications

7. Can build mobile applications

8. Electronics

Did you know?

- Whenever you see validation errors on a form, use Google Maps, watch YouTube videos, see notifications pop up, you can bet your boots that JavaScript code was written to make that happen. To put it into perspective, there are approximately 1.6 billion web sites in the world, and JavaScript is used on 95% of them. Blimey!

- JavaScript was developed by Brendan Eich

- Originally the language was called Live Script, but because Java was popular, they renamed it to 'JavaScript' mainly for marketing reasons

- Some JavaScript functionality isn't always supported on every browser. Known as 'browser incompatibilities.' This means our code can potentially break on a web page. So to solve this we have to add a 'polyfill' to make it work. A JavaScript polyfill is a piece of code used to provide functionality that isn't supported by the browser by default

TypeScript

> "But seriously, in every project I've converted, TypeScript has found bugs. And rationalizing the types leads to much clearer code."
>
> – *Tom Dale*

Language introduction

TypeScript is known as a superset of JavaScript. It contains all the features of JavaScript but has been expanded/enhanced to give more features. Any JavaScript code you write in a TypeScript file will still be valid, but you can do even more than you otherwise would not be able to do in JavaScript. Regardless, TypeScript compiles it down to JavaScript eventually when it's served on a website.

Code example

Depending on the browser, JavaScript features may or may not be available. If they are not available, it could break our application. But we want to use new features when we do development, and we also want to be strict with what we build. I want to ensure that the URL in the example below is of type 'string' and I can shape what data each post will have when I loop through them and output their title.

 **get-posts.ts**

```
interface Post {
  userId: string;
  id: string;
```

90

```typescript
  title: string;
  body: string;
}


async function getPosts() {
  const URL: string = "https://jsonplaceholder.typicode.com/posts";
  const response = await fetch(URL);
  response.json().then((posts: Array<Post>) => {
    posts.map((post: Post) => console.log(post.title));
  });
}
```

When I transpile the TypeScript, it will generate the JavaScript code below.

📄 **get-posts.js**

```javascript
"use strict";
async function getPosts() {
  const URL = "https://jsonplaceholder.typicode.com/posts";
  const response = await fetch(URL);
  response.json().then(posts => {
    posts.map(post => console.log(post.title));
  });
}
```

If I were to make a mistake and assign URL the integer value '22', it would stop me from generating the JavaScript and highlight that it's the wrong data type. This is a common issue that goes unnoticed at times when TypeScript is not there to 'type check' your code for you.

📃 **get-posts.ts**

```ts
const URL: string = 22;
// Error! Type '22' is not assignable to type 'string'
```

JavaScript is dynamically typed, meaning it doesn't strictly set it's variables like TypeScript does. I could set the 'URL' to be a string, a number or a list of values, and it wouldn't complain.

📃 **get-posts.js**

```js
let URL = "https://jsonplaceholder.typicode.com/posts";
URL = 123;
URL = null;
URL = [9, 9, 9];
// No errors in JavaScript
```

Use cases

- Front-end developers

- Full-stack developers

- Back-end developers (Node.js)

TypeScript is equally as valuable as JavaScript and can achieve the same things.

Did you know?

- TypeScript cracked the top ten languages to use in the StackOverflow survey 2019

- It's the seventh-most used language on Github

- TypeScript is backed by Microsoft

- The framework Angular (not version one) uses TypeScript as standard

PHP

> "I've never thought of PHP as more than a simple tool to solve problems."
>
> – *Rasmus Lerdorf, creator of PHP*

Language introduction

PHP - which originally stood for Personal Home Page but now stands for PHP: Hypertext Preprocessor is a general-purpose scripting language which was originally designed to build dynamic web applications. Today, it can be used for command-line scripting but is mainly used for server-side development.

PHP code can be embedded in an HTML document by placing it between two delimiters.

```
<?php
// php code
?>
```

Code example

Here we will look at an example of a PHP script that will check if the user is logged in. If they are, then they'll see a button to view their dashboard. If they have not logged in, then we show them a log in button. This script is first executed on the server, generates the HTML and then gets sent to the client.

📄 **index.php (Server-side version)**

```php
<?php session_start(); ?>
<!DOCTYPE html>
<html>
  <head>
    <title>App</title>
  </head>
  <body>
    <header>
      <?php if (isset($_SESSION["app.co.uk"])) { ?>
        <button id="view-dashboard-button">View Dashboard</button>
      <?php } else { ?>
        <button id="log-in-button">Log in</button>
      <?php } ?>
    </header>
  </body>
</html>
```

The HTML below would be returned if I was not logged in. Take note that the PHP logic gets stripped out for the client-side version below.

📄 **index.php (Client-side version)**

```html
<!DOCTYPE html>
<html>
  <head>
    <title>App</title>
  </head>
  <body>
    <header>
      <button id="log-in-button">Log in</button>
    </header>
  </body>
</html>
```

Because PHP is server-side, it will have access to things we want to keep private from the client.

Use cases

PHP IS *EVERYWHERE!* Anything you can do on a web server, you can do with PHP. You may use it for a small personal blog or something huge like a commercial software application. It has a wide range of support for databases. twenty-three in fact. *Say whaaat!?*

PHP is used for building content management systems, E-Commerce sites, University sites, news sites, wiki sites, stock image sites, search engines and social media sites. Pretty much any type of website out there can be built with it, to be frank.

The type of developers who would use it:

- Back-end developers

- Full-stack developers

- WordPress/Drupal/Joomla developers

Did you know?

- Facebook, Wikipedia, Yahoo and Photobucket are all websites built (or originally built) with the PHP language

- Based on Wikipedia's research, 75 percent of all websites use PHP. 244+ million websites use it

- The PHP language has evolved over many years but didn't have a formal written standard/specification until 2014

- The mascot of PHP is a big blue elephant named the 'elePHPant'

- Since the release of PHP 7, websites that have upgraded from version 5.6 have seen significant improvements in speed and handling of requests

SQL

> "Structured Query Language, SQL is a domain-specific programming language that is used to communicate with a database."
>
> *– bytescout.com*

Language introduction

A database is a collection of structured data stored in electronic form on a computer system. The database gets manipulated by a database management system and SQL is the language to carry out this manipulation.

The SQL programming language can be used to cherry-pick data we are looking for (SELECT), or to modify data (UPDATE), add new data (INSERT) and to remove data (DELETE). An E-Commerce store would store many things in a database. A few examples being:

1. The entire stock of products they sell

2. The customers who've created accounts

3. The orders placed

The SQL language is used to interact with database management systems. Below are some of the examples.

1. PostgreSQL - Open Source

2. SQLite - Open Source

3. MySQL - Owned by Oracle

Code example

Please note: *This example uses the database management system MySQL/SQLite syntax.*

First, we create a table called 'products' for a grocery store. This will store a unique identifier, a product code, an identifiable name, the quantity of that item in stock, and how much it costs.

products.sql

```sql
CREATE TABLE IF NOT EXISTS products (
    productID    INT UNSIGNED  NOT NULL AUTO_INCREMENT,
    productCode  CHAR(3)       NOT NULL,
    name         VARCHAR(30)   NOT NULL,
    quantity     INT UNSIGNED  NOT NULL DEFAULT 0,
    price        DECIMAL(7,2),
    PRIMARY KEY  (productID)
);
```

Now, we insert three new products with varying quantities of fruits into our database. Mm mm.

```sql
INSERT INTO products (productCode, name, quantity, price)
    VALUES('A01', 'Apple', 100, 0.20);
INSERT INTO products (productCode, name, quantity, price)
    VALUES('B02', 'Bananas', 150, 0.25);
INSERT INTO products (productCode, name, quantity, price)
    VALUES('C03', 'Cherries', 75, 0.25);
```

Now that we have inserted them using SQL, we can retrieve them back whenever we want to show them to the customer.

```sql
SELECT productID, productCode, name, quantity, price
FROM products;
```

This will give us back all of the products we have in our 'products' table.

```
1 A01 Apple    100 0.20
2 B02 Bananas  150 0.25
3 C03 Cherries 75  0.25
```

Use cases

SQL is used by full-stack, server-side developers and database administrators (DBAs). Databases, in general, have a lot of intricacies that, if not known about, can cause huge performance issues if not understood.

Did you know?

- SQL is an international standard and recognised by ISO and ANSI standard bodies

- SQL was previously known as SEQUEL that stands for Structured English Query Language. It got changed though, as SEQUEL was a trademark of the UK based aircraft company, so it was renamed to SQL

- SQL has a strong relation to mathematics where it gets its roots from Set Theory

C

"C is quirky, flawed, and an enormous success."

– Dennis Ritchie, creator of C

Language introduction

C was born in 1969 at Bell Labs – 'The Idea Factory,' arguably the leading research organisation in Information Technology and Communications. Some consider C the most popular programming language ever created.

At one point in history – with the rise of the UNIX operating system, every programmer needed to know how to write C code. C is the basis of/influenced many other languages, including Java, JavaScript, Rust, Go, PHP, C# & C++, Python, Perl.

Code example

C is a compiled language. This means that you write C in a text file, then convert it into machine code by a process called compilation, this turns the code into another language called Assembly which is processor specific; this is then assembled (like compilation, but for Assembly) into machine code, resulting in an object file.

If there are multiple object files, these are linked together to form a larger object known as an executable which the processor can read from memory and execute.

main.c

```c
#include <stdio.h>
int main(void)
{
    printf("I've been compiled!\n");
    return (0);
}
```

I use a tool called 'GCC' (the GNU Compiler Collection) to compile, link, and assemble the C file(s) to produce an executable that we can run.

I use a command called 'ls' to list out the files in a directory. You can see it's created a new file called 'a.out.' This is the default name for a compiled file.

```
~$ gcc main.c
~$ ls
a.out main.c
```

I then run the executable file 'a.out' which is a machine code equivalent of my script 'main.c.'

```
~$ ./a.out
I've been compiled
```

Use cases

C is widely used in embedded systems, commonly found in consumer, cooking, industrial or automotive applications, but is also the basis for many high-level languages and used to build operating systems.

Did you know?

- The reason why C is so popular is because its syntax and memory model maps very well to machine instructions on many processors. This equates to very high control of the generated code and means superior performance to other languages where this is not the case

- C program execution always starts from a 'main' function. An implementation can always provide another way to enter a C program as an extension to the language

- The kernel of the popular Operating system 'Linux' is written in C

C++

> "C makes it easy to shoot yourself in the foot; C++ makes it harder, but when you do it blows your whole leg off."

> *– Bjarne Stroustrup, creator of C++*

Language introduction

C++ is an enhancement of C (discussed in the previous chapter). It was developed by Bjarne Stroustrup, a Danish computer scientist who worked on it as part of his Ph.D. project and was first standardised in 1998. Again, C++ is used literally everywhere but also for embedded systems engineering, and has a huge influence in communications and gaming. Electronic Arts' Frostbite, Crytek's CryEngine and Epic Games' Unreal engine, to name a few, are all game engines used to build AAA games.

Code example

C & C++ share similar syntax (conventions of language and grammar), but neither is a superset of the other. The main difference is that C is procedural, where C++ can be procedural, object-oriented and more. These are styles/paradigms of solving programming problems.

As I write this, I'm ordering dog food, so I thought this might be a good example of a real life object. So let's build a class. In C++, each class has two files. The header file 'DogFood.h' which contains a list of the definitions (e.g. 'cost') and functions 'getCost,' 'applyDiscount.'

📑 DogFood.h

```cpp
#pragma once
class DogFood
{
private:
  double cost;

public:
  DogFood(double cost);
  ~DogFood();
  double getCost();
  void applyDiscount(double discount);
};
```

We will import the associated header file below in our 'DogFood' source file.

📑 DogFood.cpp

```cpp
#include <iostream>
#include "DogFood.h"

using namespace std;

DogFood::DogFood(double cost)
{
  this->cost = cost;
  cout << "Created dog food with cost of " << cost << endl;
}

DogFood::~DogFood()
{
  cout << " Destroyed DogFood object" << endl;
}

double DogFood::getCost()
{
  return this->cost;
}
```

```cpp
void DogFood::applyDiscount(double discount)
{
    this->cost -= discount;
    cout << "Applying discount of " << discount << endl;
}
```

Then finally we have the main source file that gets run. Here is where we create a new dog food object, apply a discount of £10, and then output the total cost. Bargain!

📄 Main.cpp

```cpp
#include <iostream>
#include "DogFood.h"

using namespace std;

int main()
{
    double dogFoodCost = 39.99;
    DogFood dogFood{dogFoodCost};
    dogFood.applyDiscount(10);
    double cost = dogFood.getCost();

    cout << "Total cost with discount: " << cost << endl;
}
```

We create a new 'DogFood' object and pass the initial cost. We then apply a discount, then we retrieve the cost and output the result. Here is the output.

```
OUTPUT:
Created dog food with cost of 39.990000
Applying discount of 10
Total cost with discount: 29.99
Destroyed DogFood object
```

C++ doesn't have garbage collection (automatic memory management), so you should manage memory by yourself. It may look scary, but you can avoid most of the problems using modern C++ features.

Use cases

C++ is adopted in many areas for writing huge real-time critical systems due to its high performance, portable distribution, and proper resource utilisation.

1. Embedded systems

2. Architecture CAD drawing

3. 3D Modelling

4. AAA Games and Game Engine development

5. Production control software

6. Supply chain management software

7. Ticket search engines

8. Transaction networks (VISA, Mastercard, AMEX)

9. Finance such as big banks, Hedge funds and Exchanges

10. Used in Academia in many areas such as physics, but also machine learning and molecular dynamics

C++ is pretty much used everywhere.

Did you know?

•   Many programming languages are influenced by C++, some of which are C#, Java and newer versions of C

•   The success of C++ is that it supports various programming styles/paradigms

- C and C++ were both invented at Bell Laboratories.

C Sharp

Language introduction

Similar to C++, C# (pronounced "See-sharp") is a modern object-oriented programming language developed in 2000. Microsoft created C# so they could have control of their own source code. It's one of the most popular programming languages in the world.

Unlike C++, C# does clean up after itself. When putting data in memory, once you've finished with it, C# knows to remove that data once it isn't needed anymore – this is referred to as garbage collection.

Garbage collection

Imagine putting some furniture in a sitting room. If you kept putting more and more in the room, eventually you would run out of space. So the old furniture you don't need anymore needs to be taken out to free up space. The same happens with the memory storage on your computer.

Code example

Here we have a collection of sofas, and we ask the user to choose a sofa to remove from the room. Once all the sofas have been removed, the program will end. Those damn Bailiffs...

📄 FurnitureProgram.cs

```csharp
using System;
using System.Collections.Generic;
using System.Linq;

class FurnitureProgram
{
    static void Main(string[] args)
    {
        const int NO_FURNITURE_LEFT = 0;
        List<string> furniture;
        furniture = new List<string> {
            "Black sofa",
            "Grey Armchair",
            "Blue Ottoman Sofa",
            "Purple Daybed",
            "Yellow Camelback Sofa"
        };

        while (furniture.Count != NO_FURNITURE_LEFT)
        {
            furniture.ForEach(item =>
            {
                Console.Write(
                    "{0}\n",
                    furniture.IndexOf(item) + ". " + item
                );
            });
            Console.Write(
                "\n{0}",
                "Which piece of furniture should we take? "
            );
            int choiceIndex = int.Parse(Console.ReadLine());
            string choice = furniture.ElementAt(choiceIndex);
            Console.Write("\n{0} ", "Removed: " + choice);
            furniture.RemoveAt(choiceIndex);
```

```
    }

    Console.Write("\n{0}", "Your room is kind of empty now...");
  }
}
```

Here is the output of the program when executing the script above.

```
0. Black sofa
1. Grey Armchair
2. Blue Ottoman Sofa
3. Purple Daybed
4. Yellow Camelback Sofa

Which piece of furniture should we remove from your room? 0

Removed: Black sofa

... And so on.

0. Yellow Camelback Sofa

Which piece of furniture should we remove from your room? 0

Removed: Yellow Camelback Sofa

Your room is kind of empty now...
```

Use cases

C# is one of the go-to programming languages for creating games. A game engine called Unity – the de-facto of most game studios – makes wide use of C# to build anything from small side-scrolling games to immersive Virtual Reality (VR) experiences.

C# is also heavily used in the Microsoft ecosystem to build Windows applications and web applications.

Did you know?

- Microsoft gave programming language designer Anders Hejlsberg the task of creating a "better Java." This resulted in the birth of C# and the .NET framework

- Microsoft first used the name C# in 1988

- C# is a very in-demand skill. It's considered the 4th most popular programming language, with the third largest community on StackOverflow

Java

> "Java is C++ without the guns, clubs and knives."
>
> *– James Gosling, creator of Java*

Language introduction

Java is used by 90% of Fortune 500 companies as their server-side language. It's the official and original language for development with the Android platform. From laptops to data centres, game consoles and scientific computers use it. It exists in a lot of places.

Java is an object-oriented language like C++ and C#.

Code example

In the Investment world, a customer can create as many pots as they'd like. So if the back-end engineers create an 'Investment Pot' class, it can be used again and again to model pots of a real customer.

Here is a contrived example of an Investment Pot.

📄 InvestmentPot.java

```java
class InvestmentPot {
  private float total;

  public InvestmentPot(float total) {
    this.total = total;
  }

  public void addContribution(float contribution) {
    // add the new contribution to the total cash pot value
```

```java
    this.total += contribution;
  }

  public String outputTotal() {
    return "Total pot value is " + this.total;
  }
}
```

Above the pot can store the total cash amount that a pot has, and we have exposed a behaviour/method/function that allows people to add more money/make a contribution.

We usually have a main entry-point into the application. The code below will be fired first when running the application.

📄 **App.java**

```java
public class App {
  public static void main(String[] args) {
    float startingAmount = 2000;
    float contribution = 250;
    // We are creating a new object of
    // our InvestmentPot class blueprint
    InvestmentPot myPot = new InvestmentPot(startingAmount);
    // calling the method below
    myPot.addContribution(contribution);

    System.out.print(myPot.outputTotal());
  }
}
```

Here is the output.

```
OUTPUT:
Total pot value is 2250.0
```

Use cases

Java is extremely popular. There are more than nine million Java developers in the world and the odds of getting a job are quite high. According to indeed.com, Java is the top language for job postings.

• Build Android apps

• Build software tools

• Enterprise applications

• Used by NASA (One application zooms in from outer space and can examine a location on earth)

• Used for self-driving cars

• Math-oriented applications (Scientific processing with visualisers)

• One of the main choices of Academic study for Computer science

Did you know?

• Java was created back in 1995 - meaning it's one of the oldest programming languages in motion

• Java gets downloaded more than a billion times each year

• Java's original name was OAK. The creator James Gosling named it after the oak tree he saw outside his office window

• Google and Oracle had to settle a $9 billion copyright lawsuit around the use of Java – a language owned by Oracle. Google had incorporated 11,500 lines of Oracle's code into the Android platform

Python

> "Python is an experiment in how much freedom programmers need. Too much freedom and nobody can read another's code; too little and expressiveness is endangered."
>
> – *Guido van Rossum, creator of Python*

Language introduction

Python was created in 1991. It's considered a high-level general-purpose programming language that is used a lot for crunching data. It can be used for building desktop applications, websites and web applications. It has an enormous selection of libraries which aid in many areas of expertise such as astronomy, mathematics, science computation, image processing, and even deep/machine learning.

Code example

Here is an example of a script that finds the mean, median and variance of weekly book sales. Ahh man, I *wish* it was real data of this book. Oh well, a man can dream.

 **weekly-book-sales.py**

```python
import statistics

weekly_book_sales = [205, 221, 175, 228, 248, 487, 124, 253, 227, 241, 226,
497, 285, 194, 373, 343, 220, 447, 482, 194, 489, 426, 289, 277, 317, 178,
355, 106]
```

```
print(statistics.mean(weekly_book_sales))
print(statistics.median(weekly_book_sales))
print(statistics.variance(weekly_book_sales))
```

Here is the output.

```
OUTPUT:
289.5357142857143 - mean
250.5 - median
13187.072751322752 - variance
```

Use cases

Data scientists use it to understand patterns/trends in data. Understanding data is vital in many industries, for example:

1. Biology (DNA analysis, soil samples, proteins & genetics)

2. Insurance (claim prediction)

3. Retail banking (Market analysis and Cryptocurrency)

4. Hardware (Robotics)

5. Aerospace (Simulation)

6. Finance (Algorithmic Trading, Volatility prediction)

7. Healthcare (Drug discovery, Treatment decisions and Prognosis)

8. Meteorology (Weather forecasting)

A full list of Python's success stories can be found here https://www.python.org/about/success. It's truly amazing how much Python impacts the world.

Did you know?

- Python is used by Wikipedia, Dropbox, Google, YouTube, Instagram, Spotify and Reddit

- Google use it for their Search engine

- The language's name came from the sketch comedy 'Monty Python's Flying Circus'

Ruby

> "I believe that the purpose of life is, at least in part, to be happy. Based on this belief, Ruby is designed to make programming not only easy but also fun. It allows you to concentrate on the creative side of programming, with less stress."
>
> *– Yukihiro Matsumoto, Creator of Ruby*

Language introduction

Ruby was built in such a way that it allows the software to be understood by humans first and computers second. It was created by Yukihiro Matsumoto and publicly released in 1995. Since it's release, it has achieved a massive following, perhaps due to it being considered productive, flexible and fun to work with.

Code example

Our code example will take a list of flying passengers and pass them through security control. I'm flying to Morocco tomorrow, so this code example will make sure I pack my passport tonight and put my liquids in those tiny little plastic bags. *They're TOO small!*

First, I'll create a 'Passenger' class that passes in: a name, whether they do or do not have their passport, and a total measure in millilitres of all the liquids they are carrying.

 **passengers.rb**

```ruby
class Passenger
  attr_accessor :name, :has_passport, :total_liquids_in_ml

  def initialize(name, has_passport, total_liquids_in_ml)
    @name = name
    @has_passport = has_passport
    @total_liquids_in_ml = total_liquids_in_ml
  end
end
```

Now, we are saying we only accept a maximum of 100ml. Each passenger will be passed through a security check function.

```ruby
MAX_LIQUID_ML = 100

def security_check(passenger)
  if passenger.has_passport == false
    puts "Passenger #{passenger.name} cannot board plane"
  elsif passenger.total_liquids_in_ml > MAX_LIQUID_ML
    puts "Passenger #{passenger.name} bin some liquids, please"
  else
    puts "Passenger #{passenger.name} passed checks"
  end
end
```

Next, we create each of our passengers, then run each passenger through the security check above.

```ruby
passengers = []

passengers.push Passenger.new('Fred', true, 60)
passengers.push Passenger.new('Wilma', true, 120)
passengers.push Passenger.new('Barney', false, 40)
passengers.push Passenger.new('Betty', true, 95)
passengers.push Passenger.new('Gazoo', false, 0)
passengers.push Passenger.new('Mr Slate', true, 10)
```

```
# security check applied for each
passengers.each { |passenger| security_check(passenger) }
```

Here is the output.

```
OUTPUT:
Passenger Fred passed checks
Passenger Wilma bin some liquids, please
Passenger Barney cannot board plane
Passenger Betty passed checks
Passenger Gazoo cannot board plane
Passenger Mr Slate passed checks
```

Use cases

Full-stack developers and back-end developers would make use of Ruby. It was designed as a general-purpose scripting language but is mainly used for web applications, simple libraries and servers. Ruby on Rails is the web server-side framework that sits on top of Ruby to build such web applications.

Did you know?

• Twitter, GitHub, AirBnb, Instacard and Cookpad are examples of big sites that were built upon the Ruby language

• The creator Yukihiro 'Matz' Matsumoto blended parts of his favourite languages (Perl, Smalltalk, Eiffel, Ada and Lisp) to form Ruby

• The name Ruby originated from an online chat session between Matsumoto and Keiju Ishitsuka in 1993

Rust

"The fact that Rust continues to mature is incredibly exciting."

– *Ivan Ristic, security expert and author*

Language introduction

Rust was born as a personal project by Graydon Hoare in 2006. It's a language that is used to build the Firefox web browser, a few Operating systems, high-performance servers and also used for embedded systems. Rust is considered a safer alternative to the C language because of the way it manages system memory.

Its benefits are:

1. Safety – Unlikely to have memory-related bugs; prevents some types of threading bugs

2. Speed – Rust programs have comparable performance to similar C and C++ programs

3. Concurrency – Rust programs use native threads effectively

4. Cross-platform – Works on Linux, Windows, MacOS and many embedded devices

Code example

 name.rs

```rust
struct Person<'a> {
    first_name: &'a str,
    middle_names: &'a [&'a str],
    last_name: &'a str,
}

fn main() {
    let p = Person {
        first_name: "Shaun",
        middle_names: &["Michael", "Kenneth"],
        last_name: "Stone",
    };
    println!(
        "What?! You have two middle names, {} {} {}?",
        p.first_name,
        p.middle_names.join(" "),
        p.last_name
    );
}
```

Here is the output.

```
OUTPUT:
What?! You have two middle names, Shaun Michael Kenneth Stone?
```

Yes… yes, I do.

Did you know?

- The popular StackOverflow survey has voted Rust the most-loved language by developers from 2016 to 2019

- Dropbox uses Rust for its core file storage system to serve over 500 million users

- Deliveroo uses Rust to make assignment decisions in its food delivery network

Kotlin

> "A bunch of Universities have been (and others starting) using Kotlin to teach programming and other topics. Very exciting to see this grow."
>
> – *Hadi Hariri, VP of Developer Advocacy at JetBrains*

Language introduction

Kotlin is a language introduced in 2011 by a company called Jetbrains, who build tools for software developers and project managers. Kotlin is becoming the go-to programming language for building native mobile apps on the Android platform. It has been made the official Android language, meaning more students and developers from a Java background are gravitating towards it.

Code example

Kotlin is used as a new alternative to Java and is very popular with Mobile engineers of the Android platform because it has a few nice extended features and can reduce the volume of code that has to be written. Here is an example to demonstrate creating a Lamborghini vehicle.

📄 **JavaExample.java**

```
public abstract class Vehicle {
    private String name;
    Vehicle(String name){
        this.name = name;
    }
}
```

```
}
public class Lamborghini extends Vehicle {
    private String model;
    private String color;

    Lamborghini(String model, String color) {
        super("Lamborghini");
        this.model = model;
        this.color = color;
    }
}
Lamborghini aventador = new Lamborghini("Aventador", "black")
```

In the Kotlin language to achieve the same thing.

 KotlinExample.kt

```
abstract class Vehicle(val name: String)

class Lamborghini(val model: String, val color: String) :
Vehicle("Lamborghini")

val aventador = Lamborghini("Aventador", "black")
```

If only it was quicker to save up for one of these cars than it is to type this code.

Use cases

Predominantly used by Android engineers. Kotlin would power apps that are designed around (to name a few):

1.   Business

2.   Education

3.   Lifestyle

4.   Entertainment

5. Utilities

6. Productivity

7. Finances

You can also use Kotlin for front-end and back-end development, however, this is uncommon.

Did you know?

- Netflix, Uber, Atlassian, Pinterest, Coursera, Trello, Nutmeg and Evernote have written either all or part of their Android apps in Kotlin

- Google announced in 2017 that it would officially support Kotlin for the Android platform

Golang

> "Go really feels like the 'C' for the 21st century."
>
> — *Petr Hošek*

Language introduction

Go – or Golang – was created by three people at Google and first appeared in 2009. The creators are Robert Griesemer, Rob Pike and Ken Thomson. The guiding principles underlying Go involve simplicity, readability, and productivity. The code syntax is similar to C, but unlike C, it manages memory safely and is built with concurrency and parallelism in mind. *These terms are explained in Part 2 under 'Software Development Terminology.'*

Code example

 main.go

```go
package main

import (
  "fmt"
  "log"
  "net/http"
)

func handler(w http.ResponseWriter, r *http.Request) {
  // I will get the first URL segment to complete the sentence
  fmt.Fprintf(w, "Software engineers do %s now?", r.URL.Path[1:])
}

func main() {
```

```
    http.HandleFunc("/", handler)
    log.Fatal(http.ListenAndServe(":8080", nil))
}
```

Go's web servers automatically employ concurrency, which can be great for heavy traffic loads. If I run this server on my own machine and then open it in my browser, I should get a response.

```
http://localhost:8080/what
```

The segment 'what' in the URL will be read and the browser web page returns:

```
Software engineers do what now?
```

Use cases

Most Golang projects are designed with server-side development in mind. This involves web applications with concurrent connections, socket servers like streaming media, games or clients connecting to multiple servers.

Uber use Golang for handling high volumes of geofence-based queries. An example of GeoFencing will be if the driver of an Uber car is in close proximity to a passenger they are picking up on a map (by making use of GPS or RFID), a push notification gets sent to the passenger to inform them that the driver will be arriving soon. Clever stuff.

- Web apps

- Simple scripting

- System administration

- Image processing

- Cryptocurrency

- Embedded systems

Did you know?

- Companies that have embraced Golang include BBC, Twitter, Facebook, Apple, Dropbox, The New York Times and IBM.

- It broke into the top ten programming languages in the world in just three years

- It started out as a server-side language but is now considered for applications in web programming, desktop, robotics, machine learning, cloud and numerical computing

Swift

"We are willing to make the internal
implementation of Swift complex if that means
that we get a beautiful model for programmers –
one that preserves the virtues of safety-by-default,
predictability, performance, and joy-to-develop-in."

– Chris Lattner, main author of Swift

Language introduction

Swift is an open-source language that was originally developed by Apple in 2014. They encourage the use of Swift over the existing Objective-C programming language which used to be the standard for development on their own platforms.

Swift takes inspiration/incorporates aspects of Python, Rust and Ruby. A strong positive of Swift is it can be quite friendly to new programmers who want to get up and running, and due to being open for all, it's acquired a large supportive community.

Code example

In this code example, we will have a list of potential prizes, with the chance of not winning anything. I mean, the odds look pretty good. We will randomly choose one of the five possibilities. We'll then get a friendly person to announce what has been won.

Please note: *This code is not idiomatic Swift and would usually be written to work alongside Apple's tools & API libraries.*

📄 prize.swift

```swift
import Foundation

enum Prize: String, CaseIterable {
  case iphone
  case ipad
  case macbook
  case imac
  case nothing
}


let prizes: [Prize] = Prize.allCases

func pickRandomPrize(prizes: [Prize]) -> Prize {
  let randomPrize: Prize = prizes.randomElement()!
  return randomPrize
}

class PrizeAnnouncer {
  let prizeWon: Prize;
  init(prizeWon: Prize) {
      self.prizeWon = prizeWon
  }
  func announce() {
    if prizeWon == Prize.NOTHING {
        return print("You've won... nothing")
    }

    print("Congratulations! You've won an \(prizeWon)")
  }
}

let randomPrize = pickRandomPrize(prizes: prizes)
let announcer = PrizeAnnouncer(prizeWon: randomPrize)
announcer.announce()
```

Here is the result of running it five times.

```
OUTPUT:
You have won... nothing
Congratulations! You have won an iphone
Congratulations! You have won an ipad
```

```
You have won... nothing
Congratulations! You have won an imac
```

Not bad going, eh? (Wink face)

Use cases

Swift is used by Mobile and App developers of the Apple platforms. Conventionally, developers will use XCode (the software used to write code and emulate the apps on Apple devices).

Swift is most common language for any Apple software engineer working on the following platforms:

- iOS for Mobile development

- macOS for Desktop development

- watchOS for Smartwatch development

- tvOS for TV development

Did you know?

- Swift remained in development for four years in secrecy, so no-one outside of Apple knew about it during such time

- App crashes in Swift are considered lower compared to Objective C, because most of the errors are caught during the build/compilation process

- Swift is a functional, protocol-oriented and object-oriented programming language

Haxe

> "Haxe is like magic. Developers can publish native apps and games to every major platform without hassle."
>
> *– Jonathan Chung, CEO, Stencyl*

Language introduction

Haxe began in 2005 and was developed by Nicolas Cannasse (met him at a meetup once). The language is influenced by ActionScript, a language that was the de-facto for building flash games. When Steve Jobs pulled the plug on Flash support and essentially killed the Flash platform, Haxe was an option to game developers to build for mobile, desktop, and the web with one single codebase.

I have special love for Haxe. I built my first commercial mobile game with it called Ronnie the Rooster. The key selling point for me at the time was the targeting of many platforms with one codebase. I wanted my game to be compatible with Android, iOS and the web. It sure was.

Normally you would have to code the game in the native languages for each platform (Android + Java/Kotlin, iOS & Swift, web and JavaScript), which would likely take three times longer in development time. With Haxe, I could feed three birds with one scone. See what I did there?

Code example

Please note: *This example was taken from haxe.org because it's a great one that demonstrates some nice features of the language.*

rock-paper-scissors.hx

```haxe
class Game {
  static function main() {
    var playerA = {name: "Shaun the Sheep", move: Paper}
    var playerB = {name: "Bitzer the Dog", move: Rock}

    var result = switch [playerA.move, playerB.move] {
      case
        [Rock, Scissors] |
        [Paper, Rock] |
        [Scissors, Paper]: Winner(playerA);

      case
        [Rock, Paper] |
        [Paper, Scissors] |
        [Scissors, Rock]: Winner(playerB);

      case _: Draw;
    }
    trace('result: $result');
  }
}

typedef Player = {name:String, move:Move}

enum Move {
  Rock;
  Paper;
  Scissors;
}

enum Result {
  Winner(player:Player);
  Draw;
}
```

Here is the output.

```
OUTPUT:
result: Winner({ name : Shaun the Sheep, move : Paper })
```

134

Use cases

Haxe can be used to target pretty much any language but is predominantly used by games studios to create cross-platform games.

Haxe can also be used for web development because it adds more language features but transpiles to JavaScript. A similar concept to the use case of TypeScript mentioned in a previous chapter.

You can also build desktop applications with the use of something like node WebKit or Java Swing.

Did you know?

- Haxe has partnered with Gamesys, a company I used to work for back in 2017

- Haxe is used by the BBC, Nickelodeon, Hasbro, Coca-cola, Toyota, Disney, among others, ranging from small independent companies to large corporate teams

- Haxe can target Flash, JavaScript, PHP, C++, Java, C#, Python, Lua and Neko

Libraries & frameworks

Here we will look at a handful of libraries and frameworks used for the web.

- React - *Written in JavaScript*

- Vue - *Written in JavaScript*

- Angular - *Written in JavaScript*

- MVC Frameworks - *Written in various languages*

- Node.js & npm - *Written in JavaScript*

React

"The Facebook codebase has over 20,000 React components, and that's not even counting React Native."

– Dan Abramov, *software engineer at Facebook*

Language introduction

React is a JavaScript library for building visual user interfaces. These user interfaces are broken down into React components. Think of a component as a reusable lego piece that can be used to build a lego model of any size.

Examples of a component would be a button. This button can be reused for many pages, whether you are submitting a form or accepting some terms and conditions.

Web applications are usually built as a Single Page Application (SPA). What this means is it's built with the idea of not having to reload the web page when you move to another view/page, providing a more seamless experience.

As discussed in one of the first chapters, we use HTML and JavaScript. React essentially mixes these two disciplines to give control over adding/removing/manipulating markup with JavaScript.

Code example

We want to create a reusable button that can be used across all of our web applications. Thinking in this way means we are less likely to rewrite code to do the same thing.

📄 **Button.js**

```
import React from "react";

const Button = ({ children, ...otherProps }) => (
  <button className="button" {...otherProps}>
    {children}
  </button>
);

export { Button as default };
```

In the example below when we click the Button to log in, we change the text to say 'Logging in...'

📄 **Login.js**

```
import React, { useState } from "react";
import Button from "./Button";

const Login = () => {

  const [isLoggingIn, setIsLoggingIn] = useState(false);

  return (
    <>
      <h1>Log in</h1>
      <fieldset>
        <label for="email">Email:</label>
```

```
    <input
      aria-label="Enter your email"
      aria-required="true"
      type="text"
      name="email"
    />
    <label for="password">Password:</label>
    <input
      aria-label="Enter your password"
      aria-required="true"
      type="text"
      name="password"
    />
  </fieldset>
  <Button onClick={() => setIsLoggingIn(true)}>{isLoggingIn ? 'Logging
in...' : 'Log in'}</Button>
    </>
  );
);
```

Now we have a button component that can be reused for other
scenarios – not just logging in. Over time we can improve this button
component to support our brand. Maybe you want a small and large
version, therefore, we would add to the code of Button.js. The
important thing is that whenever we use a button anywhere, it will
reference this one.

React Native

React Native is a way to build native applications for iOS and
Android. It uses JavaScript, but instead of targeting the browser, it
targets mobile platforms. A lot of companies use React Native to build
their mobile applications when they don't want to invest in two teams
that are specialised in Swift for iOS as well as Java/Kotlin for Android.
Facebook, Bloomberg, Uber, Salesforce, Skyscanner and TaskRabbit

are already using it for their native applications on the Google Play and App Store.

Use cases

Front-end and full-stack developers make heavy use of React (among other libraries) to build their web applications. If done right, it helps to scale web applications, share common functionality and makes things easier to maintain.

We are using React at Nutmeg as part of our migration from a legacy web application.

Did you know?

- Jordan Walke, a software engineer at Facebook, created React

- React first deployed on Facebook's newsfeed in 2011 and on Instagram.com in 2012

- Instagram was the first 'external' user of React

- PayPal, Netflix, BBC, Nutmeg and Yahoo all use React to build their web applications

- There are two million open-source repositories on GitHub that depend on React's Facebook

Vue

> "I also really care about the approachability part of Vue, which is rooted in the belief that technology should be enabling more people to build things."
>
> – *Evan You, creator of Vue*

Language introduction

Vue.js is a UI framework. Everything is built with components in mind. Vue.js was created by Evan You, where he and active core team members maintain the project. After working for Google and making use of AngularJS in a few projects, he decided to extract the bits he liked from it but build something a bit more lightweight.

Code example

Here is an example of outputting a list of personal training plans for a gym called GymSharks.

Please note: *This implementation is based on the example taken from VueSchool.*

 app.js

```js
const PersonalTrainingPlan = {
  template: "#plan",
  props: {
    name: {
      type: String,
      required: true
```

```
    }
  }
};

const ChooseAPlan = {
  template: "#choose-a-plan",
  components: {
    plan: PersonalTrainingPlan
  },
  data() {
    return {
      plans: ["Full body", "Lower body", "Gutbuster"]
    };
  }
};

new Vue({
  el: "#app",
  components: {
    "choose-a-plan": ChooseAPlan
  }
});
```

📄 index.html

```
<!DOCTYPE html>
<html lang="en">
  <head>
    <meta charset="UTF-8" />
    <meta name="viewport" content="width=device-width, initial-scale=1.0" />
    <meta http-equiv="X-UA-Compatible" content="ie=edge" />
    <title>GymSharks</title>
  </head>
  <body>
    <!-- Application -->
    <div id="app">
      <h1>List of our Personal Training Plans</h1>
      <choose-a-plan></choose-a-plan>
    </div>
```

```
<!-- List of Plans -->
<script type="text/x-template" id="choose-a-plan">
  <ol class="plans">
    <plan v-for="plan in plans" :name="plan"></plan>
  </ol>
</script>

<!-- Plan Item -->
<script type="text/x-template" id="plan">
  <li class="plan-item">
    {{ name }}
  </li>
</script>

    <script src="https://unpkg.com/vue"></script>
    <script src="app.js"></script>
  </body>
</html>
```

When I open the browser, I should see my list of personal plans.

List of our Personal Training Plans

1. Full body
2. Lower body
3. Gutbuster

Use cases

Front-end and full-stack developers make use of Vue.js on the front-end with templates/components to build user interfaces. It's used to build highly-scalable and maintainable web applications using a 'component-driven' approach.

Did you know?

- Vue.js is used by Alibaba, WizzAir, Behance, EuroNews, Grammarly, Laracasts and GitLab, to name a few

- It receives over one million downloads a week on npm

Angular

> "Angular is built by a team of engineers who share a passion for making web development feel effortless. We believe that writing beautiful apps should be joyful and fun. We're building a platform for the future."
>
> – *angular.io*

Language introduction

The Angular framework has quite a history behind it. Version one – known as AngularJS – was created as a side project by Miško Hevery, where it was eventually embraced by Google and a wider community. There was a time where AngularJS was the most sought after skill as a front-end developer. Companies ranging from start-ups to large corporations built their web apps with it.

What was the problem? Well, the original implementation was never really thought about in terms of scalability, and businesses were identifying performance problems as their apps grew. The core team of Angular did what they could to try and alleviate this, but reached a limit of what was possible. A bombshell dropped. Angular 2.0 would be a complete rewrite, and all of the code of apps written in AngularJS (version 1) would have to be scrapped and rewritten in the new way.

No backwards compatibility

> "I work for a moderately large company (2,000 people) and were rolling out a new web experience

to replace all our old text based systems this weekend. I've backed angular the whole way and its been lovely to work with - the entire UI is written in it. This news is incredibly unfortunate, inconvenient and potentially expensive."

– Reddit user, 2014

AngularJS from July 1, 2018, was put on a three year long term support period. There was no migration strategy, so developers decided to jump in and begin the rewrite of the new Angular on top of a beta release – meaning at the time the framework was undergoing testing and wasn't officially released.

Beta software is subject to change, so this was a risky endeavour. Fast forward to the present day, where the Angular framework has now begun to stabilise and at the time of writing is on version 9.

Code example

This example is written with version 8 and will output a list of vegan recipes. Did I mention I was… actually, forget it. To simplify the code, I use a recipe name and an associated star rating of that recipe. TypeScript is used as the basis for scripting.

Here is the HTML template of my new component called 'recipe-list.'

 **app/recipe-list/recipe-list.component.html**

```html
<h1>Recipes</h1>

<ul class="recipes">
  <li class="recipe" *ngFor="let recipe of recipes">
    <h2>{{ recipe.name }}</h2>
    <p class="rating"><span>{{ recipe.starRating }}</span>/10</p>
```

```
        </li>
    </ul>
```

Here is the CSS styling of my component.

app/recipe-list/recipe-list.component.css

```css
.recipes {
  list-style: none;
  padding: 0;
}

.recipe {
  padding: 1rem;
  margin: 0;
  display: flex;
  justify-content: space-between;
  align-items: center;
}

.recipe:hover {
  background-color: #cccccc;
}

.rating {
  background-color: #e2e2e2;
  border-radius: 50%;
  margin: 0;
  padding: 1rem;
  text-align: center;
}

.rating span {
  font-size: 1.5rem;
  font-weight: bold;
}
```

We will read the recipes data from this file and feed it into our
component.

📄 **app/recipe-list/recipes.ts**

```typescript
export const recipes = [
  {
    name: "Chickpea Curry",
    starRating: 5
  },
  {
    name: "Lentil Stew",
    starRating: 4
  },
  {
    name: "Tofu Stir Fry",
    starRating: 4
  },
  {
    name: "Black bean Chilli",
    starRating: 5
  },
  {
    name: "Thai green curry",
    starRating: 3
  },
  {
    name: "Pie & Mash",
    starRating: 5
  }
];
```

Here is the associated TypeScript of my component. We import the 'recipes' file.

📄 **app/recipe-list/recipe-list.component.ts**

```typescript
import { Component } from "@angular/core";
```

```javascript
import { recipes } from "./recipes";

@Component({
  selector: "app-recipe-list",
  templateUrl: "./recipe-list.component.html",
  styleUrls: ["./recipe-list.component.css"]
})
export class RecipeListComponent {
  recipes = recipes;
}
```

Angular bootstraps the presentation, styling and functionality and bundles it as a reusable component. For any page we want to output a list of recipes, we do the following. In our 'app' component, we can inject our component selector 'app-recipe-list' to make it appear on the page.

📃 app/app.component.html

```html
<div class="app" role="main">
  <app-recipe-list></app-recipe-list>
</div>
```

Here is how it looks when we start up the app and view it in a browser.

Recipes

Chickpea Curry	5/10
Lentil Stew	4/10
Tofu Stir Fry	4/10
Black bean Chilli	5/10
Thai green curry	3/10
Pie & Mash	5/10

Use cases

Front-end and full-stack developers, as well as web designers, make use of Angular on the front-end with templates/components to build user interfaces.

Did you know?

- Angular is supported by Google

- Angular was used to build web applications for many Google products such as Google Domains and Google Marketing

Platform, AdWords and Assistant. Microsoft projects such as Microsoft Office Home, Xbox and Support. Forbes, Santandar and Tidal. A full list can be found at https://www.madewithangular.com

- From version 9 of Angular, it – by default – makes use of a compiler known as project Ivy, a way to make apps smaller (strip out code not used), faster and easier to understand/debug

MVC Web Frameworks

"The Model-View-Controller (MVC) is an
architectural pattern that separates an application
into three main logical components: the model, the
view, and the controller."

– tutorialspoint.com

Introduction

Web frameworks are a common approach to building web
applications and provide an opinionated structure of web services,
resources and APIs. They reduce the overheads of common challenges
such as dealing with URLs, serving web templates, managing the
session of a user and database access.

A typical architecture of these frameworks is to separate code into
three areas: Model, View, Controller (MVC).

Model

Models represent knowledge. A model of something such as details of
a customer or a payment.

View

A view is a visual representation of the model. The data from the
model is passed to the view.

Controller

The controller handles actions from the user and provides model data to the view.

Example

There are many frameworks written in many languages. Python (Django), PHP (Laravel, Zend, Symfony), but for this chapter, I've decided to use Ruby on Rails for demonstration. Although they are all mostly built with the same idea in mind.

Ruby on Rails

Ruby on Rails (Rails for shorthand) is a framework built with the Ruby language that was first released in 2005. It's a way to build web applications and is arguably one of the hottest technologies in web development. It has been used as the basis for other frameworks, notably Laravel (built with PHP). Most start-ups will have built their applications with Rails in the mid-2000s.

Code example

Let's demonstrate the flow of a typical MVC application. In this example, we will store a list of Business partners in a database. When we go to the URL 'business_partners/index' of our own application, we will use a model 'BusinessPartner' that maps to a database table where it will fetch a list of partners, and then the controller will pass that data down to the view where it will loop through each of the partners and output each of their names.

The first thing I will do is create the model. It inherits from a model called 'ApplicationRecord' that already has the code we need to make calls to a database I set up earlier.

 **app/models/business_partner.rb**

```ruby
class BusinessPartner < ApplicationRecord
  # This inherits a function called `all`
  # from a parent called ApplicationRecord
end
```

Using this model I will insert some rows into the database. This is called seeding.

db/seeds.rb

```ruby
BusinessPartner.create([{ name: 'Agile Solutions' }])
BusinessPartner.create([{ name: 'Forward Planning Inc' }])
BusinessPartner.create([{ name: 'Scope creep Solutions' }])
BusinessPartner.create([{ name: 'Touch base Marketing' }])
BusinessPartner.create([{ name: 'Connect the dots Corporation' }])
BusinessPartner.create([{ name: 'Ping me that memo Limited' }])
```

I can use this model in the controller to fetch the data back from the database.

app/controllers/business_partners_controller.rb

```ruby
class BusinessPartnersController < ApplicationController
  def index
    # fetch 'all' business partner records from the database
    # I will be able to use @business_partners in my view
    @business_partners = BusinessPartner.all
  end
end
```

📄 **app/views/business_partners/index.html.erb**

```erb
<h1>Business Partners</h1>

<ul>
   <% @business_partners.each do |business_partner| %>
   <li>
     <td><%= business_partner.name %></td>
   </li>
   <% end %>
</ul>
```

Here's how it looks when I run my Rails application on a local server.

Business partners   ×   +

← → C   ⓘ localhost:3000/business_partners/index

Business Partners

- Agile Solutions
- Forward Planning Inc
- Scope creep Solutions
- Touch base Marketing
- Connect the dots Corporation
- Ping me that memo Limited

Use cases

Full-stack web developers would make use of Rails to build web applications as it involves working on back-end and front-end code as part of the framework.

Did you know?

- Rails releases new versions on Christmas day by tradition. Their latest release was 2.7.0 on 25th December 2019

- Rails is used by AirBnb, Couchsurfing, Bloomberg, Dribble, GitHub, Soundcloud, Yellow pages and SlideShare to name a few

Node.js & npm

"Node.js® is a JavaScript runtime built on Chrome's
V8 JavaScript engine."

– nodejs.org

At one point, JavaScript was only something you could run in a browser (client-side language). Node.js is an extension to that where you can run something as a standalone application. Node.js is a framework to develop server-side applications using the JavaScript language.

When you open up the CLI and type 'node', you are interacting with the node executable installed on your machine. When you pass a JavaScript file to it, the node executable executes the file. Node.js is an Event-driven I/O server-side JavaScript environment based on Google's V8 engine.

It was designed to build scalable network applications. It processes incoming requests in a loop, known as the event loop, and operates on a single thread, using non-blocking I/O calls. This allows it to support a high volume of concurrent connections.

npm

When you download Node, it optionally gets bundled with a package manager called 'npm.' It stands for node package manager and is the de-facto for managing external dependencies/libraries.

Code example

This example is taken from my other book 'Automating with Node.js.' It creates a command-line application that can be run from a terminal. As you can see, it's using the JavaScript syntax.

📄 src/nobot.js

```javascript
const nobot = require("commander");
const { version } = require("../package");

// commands
const setup = require("./commands/setup");
const game = require("./commands/game");
const template = require("./commands/template");

nobot.version(version);

nobot
  .command("setup")
  .description("clone repository dependencies")
  .action(setup);

nobot
  .command("game <ticketId>")
  .description("create and deploy a new game reskin")
  .action(game);

nobot
  .command("template")
  .description("release core files of template")
  .option("-i, --id, [id]", "what template to release")
  .action(template);

nobot.command("*").action(() => nobot.help());

nobot.parse(process.argv);

if (!process.argv.slice(2).length) {
```

```
    nobot.help();
}
```

Use cases

Node.js is ideal for real-time web applications that make use of real-time chatting, audio or video streaming. It's also used for Crowdfunding, E-Commerce, payment processing, and enterprise web services.

This would be used by full-stack or server-side developers but is also used by front-end developers to compile/bundle web applications.

Did you know?

- Netflix is the world's top supplier of video streaming for movies and TV series. They use Node.js in production to deliver over 140 million hours of high-quality video content every day

- Trello is used by over fifty million people worldwide and relies on Node.js server sides to serve these high numbers with an event-driven architecture

- PayPal was one of the first companies to swap Node.js for Java on the server-side. They saw huge improvements in doing so. They wrote 33% fewer lines of code and response time decreased by 35%

Wrap up

"Our greatest weakness lies in giving up. The most certain way to succeed is always to try just one more time."

– Thomas A. Edison

Well, there you have it. Hopefully, enough information to whet your appetite. As Thomas Edison said, keep trying. Learning something new is always difficult at first. Heck, I'm learning Spanish and it's difficult to grasp, but I'll keep trying and won't give up – vale la pena.

So, what are the next steps for you?

Next steps

1. Choose a language and either read a book or take a course to learn the essentials. *Examples of online courses and book publishers can be found below*

2. Work on a small project that allows you to demonstrate your new-found knowledge

3. If you get stuck on a project, use Google or StackOverflow to solve any errors or questions you have

4. Finish a few small-to-large projects so you can put them on your CV

5. Look for a low paid or unpaid freelance job and apply the skills you've honed

6. With some experience under your belt, write up your CV to make it relevant. Go easy on the keyword bingo!

7. Start looking for entry-level jobs and sell yourself

8. Once you've acquired interest for an open role, practice some interview questions found on the web

9. Refer to the Interview process chapter in Part 1

10. If you get the job, it's time to prove yourself!

Online course platforms

- FreeCodeCamp

- CodeAcademy

- CodeSchool

- Coursera

- Udemy

- Code.org

- Khan Academy

- edX.org

- Udacity

Trusted Book publishers

- Apress

- Manning

- Packt

- O'Reilly

- Sage

- Wiley

Cities for tech jobs

- London, UK

- Manchester, UK

- Bristol, UK

- Brighton, UK

- San Francisco, USA

- New York, USA

- Shanghai, China

- Stockholm, Sweden

- Singapore

- Hong Kong

- Bangalore, India

- Kuala Lumpur, Malaysia

- Berlin, Germany

- Melbourne, Australia

- Sydney, Australia

- Toronto, Canada

Cities for company start-ups

- London, UK

- Stockholm, Sweden

- Amsterdam, Netherlands

- Bangkok, Thailand

- Singapore

- Tel Aviv, Israel

- Tokyo, Japan

- Kuala Lumpur, Malaysia

If you have any questions, suggestions or improvements, feel free to let me know by contacting me here: http://smks.co.uk/contact

Alternatively, you can follow me on the following social networks.

- GitHub - https://github.com/smks

- Twitter - https://twitter.com/shaunmstone

- YouTube - https://www.youtube.com/c/OpenCanvas

Or connect with me on LinkedIn for business-related requests.

LinkedIn - https://www.linkedin.com/in/shaunmstone

Thank you for reading and I wish you all the best. If you enjoyed reading this book, please feel free to leave an online review.

Good luck! Over and out.

Shaun Michael Stone

www.ingramcontent.com/pod-product-compliance
Lightning Source LLC
Chambersburg PA
CBHW071131050326
40690CB00008B/1419